celebrating COBBLERS AND PIES

By

Avner Laskin

A LEISURE ARTS PUBLICATION

Vice President and Chief Operations Officer: Tom Siebenmorgen
Vice President, Sales and Marketing: Pam Stebbins
Vice President, Operations: Jim Dittrich
Editor in Chief: Susan White Sullivan
Director of Designer Relations: Debra Nettles
Senior Art Director: Rhonda Shelby
Senior Director Prepress: Mark Hawkins

Produced for Leisure Arts, Inc. by Penn Publishing Ltd.
www.penn.co.il
Editor: Deanna Linder
Culinary editing: Tamar Zakut
Design and layout: Ariane Rybski
Photography: Daniel Lailah
Food styling: Amit Farber
Special thanks to "Hafatzim" www.hafatzim.com

PRINTED IN CHINA

ISBN-13: 978-1-60900-009-7
Library of Congress Control Number: 2009943549

Cover photography by Daniel Lailah

Contents

Introduction

The most important part of both pies and cobblers is the crust – the crisp and flaky base that complements any filling. The fillings for these scrumptious desserts are numerous, from fruit-based to chocolate-based and everything in-between. Pies and cobblers are great desserts for holiday celebrations, birthday parties, or just everyday dinners at home, and when they emerge from your own oven they fill your home with a rich, heavenly aroma that captivates you and your family.

What could be more American than apple pie, more traditional than Thanksgiving pumpkin pie or Christmas cranberry pie? Pies are an important part of all of our celebrations and can be easy enough to make for everyday gatherings as well. Once you get the dough-making down, you only need to pick a filling that suits your occasion, and you've produced a perfect, classic dessert that no one can resist.

While a pie most often starts with the crust, a cobbler usually begins with the filling. Cobbler fillings can be one or more types of fruit, nuts, and even vegetables. The name derives from the cobbled look of the top crust, created by chunks of dough placed over the filling before baking. A really easy and delicious dessert for entertaining, cobblers are best served right out of the oven and paired with a cold scoop of your favorite ice cream.

In **Celebrating Cobblers and Pies** you'll find a wide variety of classic pie and cobbler recipes, along with creative new twists on the originals that will turn any ordinary occasion into a memorable event. I hope you enjoy these recipes as much as I have (along with my family and friends who were around to taste), and I encourage you to experiment with what's here to create your own custom desserts.

About the Author

Avner Laskin studied at the prestigious "Cordon Bleu Academy" in Paris, where he received the "Grand Diplôme de Cuisine and Pâtisserie". He later specialized in traditional breads under the world-renowned Jean-Louis Clément at the "Lenôtre School", also in Paris, and was awarded the coveted "Diplôme de Pain de Tradition et de Qualité" in 1998. Laskin's culinary career includes internships at two-star Michelin restaurants in France and Germany, and extensive work as a restaurant consultant—specializing in kitchen design and recipe and menu development. He is the author of several cookbooks.

Basic Recipes

Perfect Pie Dough

Almond Tart Dough

Juicy Cobbler Dough

Doughy Cobbler Dough

Pastry Cream

Caramel Sauce

Coconut Cream

Crumble (Streusel)

Almond Cream

Lemon Cream

Cream Cheese Filling

Apricot Glaze

Berry Glaze

Meringue

Perfect Pie Dough

A great dough for any pie. It is especially important not to overwork the dough while preparing it. Make sure that all your ingredients are cold, and turn off the food processor after each step.

INGREDIENTS

2 sticks (8 ounces) very cold unsalted butter, cut into cubes

¼ cup powdered sugar

1 egg

1 tablespoon cold water

½ teaspoon salt

2½ cups all-purpose flour

Note: Well wrapped, this dough can be stored in the freezer for up to two months and thawed in refrigerator.

PREPARATION

1. Put butter and powdered sugar in food processor fitted with metal blade. On pulse setting, mix for two minutes.

2. Add egg, water, and salt and pulse for another two minutes, until mixture is smooth.

3. Add flour gradually. Pulse for another minute, until mixture forms dough. Remove ball of dough from food processor, cover in plastic wrap, and refrigerate for at least one hour before use.

Almond Tart Dough

The almonds in this recipe can be substituted with an equal amount of your favorite nuts, such as walnuts, pecans, peanuts, or pistachios. Just be sure the nuts are very finely ground before you add them.

INGREDIENTS

2 sticks (8 ounces) very cold unsalted butter

$\frac{1}{2}$ cup powdered sugar

$\frac{1}{2}$ cup blanched almonds, finely ground

1 egg

2 tablespoons cold water

$\frac{1}{2}$ teaspoon salt

2 cups all-purpose flour

Note: Well wrapped, this dough can be stored in the freezer for up to two months and thawed in refrigerator.

PREPARATION

1. Put butter and $\frac{1}{4}$ cup powdered sugar in food processor fitted with a metal blade. On pulse setting, mix for two minutes.

2. Add almonds and remaining powdered sugar and pulse for another two minutes, until mixture is smooth.

3. Add egg, water, salt, and half the flour. Pulse for another two minutes, until mixture forms dough. Add remaining flour and pulse for another minute, until ball of dough is formed. Remove ball of dough from food processor, cover in plastic wrap, and refrigerate for at least an hour before use.

Variation:

To make a chocolate crust, add one tablespoon of unsweetened cocoa powder in step 2.

Juicy Cobbler Dough

This cobbler works great in recipes that call for baking fruit without cooking it first. Use it for any baked fruit pie or cobbler.

INGREDIENTS

1 stick (4 ounces) unsalted butter, cut into cubes

1 cup sugar

1 cup all-purpose flour

1 tablespoon baking powder

1 tablespoon pure vanilla extract

½ teaspoon salt

1 cup whole milk

PREPARATION

1. Using a hand or stand mixer, mix together butter and sugar on a low speed until creamy.

2. In a separate bowl, mix together flour and baking powder.

3. Add the vanilla extract, salt, milk, and half the flour mixture to mixer, continuing to mix on low speed.

4. Add remaining flour mixture and turn off mixer once dough has formed.

5. Remove ball of dough from mixer, cover in plastic wrap, and refrigerate for 20 minutes before using.

6. To use juicy cobbler dough in a recipe, scoop out chunks with a large spoon and use according to instructions.

Doughy Cobbler Dough

This cobbler works well with hard fruit that needs to be "marinated" in sugar before baking.

INGREDIENTS

1 stick (4 ounces) unsalted butter, cut into cubes

PREPARATION

1. Using a hand or stand mixer, mix together the butter and both sugars on low speed until creamy.

¼ cup sugar

¼ cup packed brown sugar

1 cup all-purpose flour

1 tablespoon baking powder

1 tablespoon pure vanilla extract

½ teaspoon salt

¼ cup boiling water

2. In a separate bowl, mix together the flour and baking powder.

3. Add the vanilla extract, salt, water and flour mixture to mixer, continuing to mix on low speed.

4. Remove ball of dough from mixer, cover in plastic wrap, and refrigerate for 20 minutes before using.

5. To use the doughy cobbler dough in a recipe, scoop out chunks with a large spoon and use according to instructions.

Pastry Cream

Makes

3

cups

Also known as Crème Patisserie or Vanilla Cream, this recipe can be used as the base for any pastry cream. Adding a touch of cinnamon, liqueur, ground ginger, ground coffee, or other flavoring can enhance this already-delicious cream.

INGREDIENTS

2 cups whole milk

½ cup sugar

6 egg yolks

1 tablespoon cornstarch

1 tablespoon flour

1 tablespoon pure vanilla extract

PREPARATION

1. In a small saucepan, bring the milk and ¼ cup of sugar to a boil.

2. Meanwhile, in medium bowl, whisk yolks together with remaining ¼ cup of sugar, cornstarch, flour, and vanilla extract until thick and well blended.

3. Once milk has reached a boil, lower heat to very low. Using whisk, gradually add egg yolk mixture, stirring constantly until bubbles appear and mixture has pudding-like consistency (about 5 minutes). Remove pan from heat at once.

4. Pour cream into clean bowl and press a piece of plastic wrap against surface to create airtight seal. Refrigerate cream until cold.

5. The pastry cream can be kept tightly covered in refrigerator for up to two days.

Caramel Sauce

Makes **1/2** cups

Pour on caramel sauce only after it has cooled to room temperature.

INGREDIENTS

1/2 cup sugar

2 tablespoons water

1 cup heavy cream

PREPARATION

1. In a medium saucepan, heat the sugar and water over medium heat until sugar dissolves and turns a golden caramel color. No stirring is necessary.

2. Lower heat and add heavy cream. Cook for about 10 minutes, stirring constantly, until sauce thickens slightly and has absorbed the sugar clusters. Remove from heat.

3. Allow caramel sauce to cool completely (about one hour), transfer to sealed container, and refrigerate. The caramel may be kept in refrigerator for up to five days.

Coconut Cream

Makes **2 1/2** cups

You can use toasted coconut for a nuttier flavor, but stick to unsweetened grated coconut for recipes with other dominant flavors.

INGREDIENTS

1 stick (4 ounces) unsalted butter, softened

1/2 cup sugar

2 eggs

PREPARATION

1. Place the butter in a heatproof bowl. Set bowl over saucepan of gently simmering water, until butter is melted. Remove bowl from pan.

⅔ cup unsweetened grated coconut

½ teaspoon pure vanilla extract

1 teaspoon dark rum

2. Whisk sugar into bowl of melted butter. Add eggs, one at a time, whisking them constantly so they don't become cooked. Whisk until mixture is well blended.

3. Mix in coconut, vanilla extract, and rum.

4. Cover bowl with plastic wrap and refrigerate for at least 30 minutes before using.

5. The coconut cream can be kept tightly covered in refrigerator for up to two days.

Crumble (Streusel)

Adding this crumble to any recipe will give your pie an old-fashioned taste and look. An added ½ teaspoon of ground allspice or cinnamon gives it extra flavor and aroma.

INGREDIENTS

1½ sticks (6 ounces) very cold unsalted butter, cut into cubes

½ cup sugar

1 egg

½ teaspoon salt

3 cups all-purpose flour

Note: Well wrapped, this dough can be stored in the freezer for up to two months and thawed in refrigerator.

PREPARATION

1. Put butter and sugar in food processor fitted with a metal blade. On pulse setting, mix for two minutes.

2. Add egg and salt and pulse for another two minutes until mixture is smooth.

3. Add flour and pulse for another minute, until mixture resembles crumbs. Remove mixture from food processor and place in sealed container in refrigerator for at least an hour before using.

Almond Cream

Makes

2½

cups

This cream is so luxurious that it can almost serve on its own as a spread.

INGREDIENTS

1 stick (4 ounces) unsalted butter, softened

½ cup sugar

2 eggs

⅔ cup blanched almonds, finely ground

½ teaspoon pure vanilla extract

1 teaspoon amaretto

PREPARATION

1. Place the butter in a heatproof bowl. Set bowl over saucepan of gently simmering water, until butter is melted. Remove bowl from pan.

2. Whisk sugar into bowl of melted butter. Add eggs, one at a time, whisking them constantly so they don't become cooked. Whisk until mixture is well blended.

3. Mix in almonds, vanilla extract, and amaretto.

4. Cover bowl with plastic wrap and refrigerate for at least 30 minutes before using.

5. The almond cream can be kept tightly covered in refrigerator for up to two days.

Lemon Cream

Makes

2

cups

If you follow two important rules, you are guaranteed a perfectly tart cream:
1. Use fresh lemons rather than substitute with preserved lemon juice.
2. Chill the cream thoroughly before use, for at least an hour in the refrigerator.

INGREDIENTS

1 cup fresh lemon juice (from about 5 lemons)

PREPARATION

1. In a small saucepan, bring the lemon juice to a boil.

½ cup sugar

4 egg yolks

1 tablespoon cornstarch

1 tablespoon flour

2. Meanwhile, in a medium bowl, whisk together the sugar, yolks, cornstarch, and flour until thick and well blended.

3. Once lemon juice has reached a boil, lower heat to very low. Using whisk, gradually add egg yolk mixture, stirring constantly, until bubbles appear and mixture has a pudding like consistency (about 5 minutes). Remove the pan from heat at once.

4. Pour cream into a clean bowl and press a piece of plastic wrap against surface to create an airtight seal. Let the cream stand until it reaches room temperature and then refrigerate.

5. The lemon cream can be kept tightly covered in refrigerator for up to two days.

Cream Cheese Filling

Makes

2½

cups

Good quality vanilla extract and cream cheese will turn this recipe into an irresistible filling you'll want to use again and again. And it doesn't require any cooking!

INGREDIENTS

½ cup powdered sugar

1 cup heavy cream

1 teaspoon pure vanilla extract

1 package (8 oz.) cream cheese

PREPARATION

1. Using a hand or stand mixer, mix together the powdered sugar, heavy cream, and vanilla extract on low speed until cream starts to thicken. Increase mixer speed as cream gains texture, and continue to beat until soft whipped cream forms.

2. Using a spatula, gently fold cream cheese into whipped cream just until combined.

3. The cream cheese can be kept covered in refrigerator for up to 24 hours. Use it while it's still cold.

Apricot Glaze

Makes **5** cups

The glaze, known in French as "napage", is very easy to make. It brightens the appearance of baked goods, giving them a fresh look, as if they were just taken out of the oven.

INGREDIENTS

1 cup water

2 tablespoons sugar

One 16-oz. can apricots (including the syrup)

3 Golden Delicious apples, coarsely chopped (with skin and core)

1 tablespoon powdered pectin

PREPARATION

1. Place the water, sugar, apricots, and apples in a large saucepan over high heat and bring to a boil.

2. Lower heat and stir in powdered pectin. Cook over low heat for about 30 minutes.

3. Press glaze through a strainer and let stand until it reaches room temperature.

4. The glaze can be kept in sealed container in refrigerator for up to 6 months.

Berry Glaze

Makes **4** cups

Especially suitable for red or purple fruit-based bakes, this glaze enhances both color and taste. Glaze a pie that's just emerged from the oven and watch it come to life!

INGREDIENTS

1 cup water

1 cup sugar

1 pound frozen mixed berries

1 tablespoon powdered pectin

PREPARATION

1. Place the water, sugar, and berries in a large saucepan over high heat and bring to a boil.

2. Lower heat and stir in powdered pectin. Cook over low heat for about 30 minutes.

3. Press glaze through a strainer and let stand until it reaches room temperature.

4. The glaze can be kept in sealed container in refrigerator for up to 6 months.

Meringue

Makes

3

cups

This meringue works well for piping decorative shapes and can be served cold or scorched using kitchen torch.

INGREDIENTS

3 egg whites

1 cup sugar

1 teaspoon cornstarch

PREPARATION

1. Using a hand or stand mixer fitted with whisk attachment, beat egg whites, starting on low speed. Once whites are soft, gradually add sugar.

2. Increase mixer speed to high and beat until stiff, glossy peaks form (about 10 minutes).

3. Add cornstarch and beat for another minute.

4. Transfer meringue to pastry bag and use as directed in recipe.

Fruits

Cinnamon Apple Pie

•

Tarte Tatin

•

Caramel Apple Pie

•

Pears in Red Wine Pie

•

Caramelized Banana Tarts

•

Apple Raisin Tart

•

Apricot Crumble

•

Passion Fruit Cream Tarts

•

Grilled Peach Tart

•

Mango and Coconut Cream Tarts

•

Plum Linzer Torte

•

Lemon Cream and Grape Tarts

•

Peach and Amaretto Cobbler

•

Nectarine Cobbler

•

Pineapple and Caramel Cobbler

•

Plum Clafoutis

•

Apple Cobbler

•

Fresh Pineapple Pie

•

Baked Lemon Tarts

•

Key Lime Tarts

•

Apple and Berry Pie

Cinnamon Apple Pie

Serves

A modern rendition of classic apple pie, this version is really easy to make and always a favorite. Serve it warm with a scoop of vanilla ice cream for the perfect match.

INGREDIENTS

1 stick (4 ounces) unsalted butter

¼ cup sugar

7 Golden Delicious apples, peeled and cored: 4 (for filling) cut into ½-inch cubes, and 3 (for top decoration) cut into thin slices

1 teaspoon cinnamon

Almond Tart Dough (page 9)

¼ cup Apricot Glaze (page 16)

2 tablespoons water

Equipment

One standard 9-inch pie plate

PREPARATION

1. Preheat oven to 375°F.

2. Heat a large skillet over medium heat and add butter and sugar. Cook until butter melts and sugar turns a light caramel color.

3. Add the 4 cubed apples and cinnamon and cook over low heat until apples have soaked up caramel liquid and are nearly dry (30-40 minutes).

4. Set apples aside to chill. They can be prepared a day in advance and refrigerated.

5. Working on a well-floured surface, roll out dough to a thickness of about ⅛ inch.

6. Carefully place sheet of dough into pie plate, using your fingers to gently press dough into bottom and up sides. Trim excess edges of dough, roll into ball, cover with plastic wrap, and freeze for future use.

7. Pour caramelized apples on top of dough. Arrange the 3 sliced apples on top of caramelized apples, starting at the edges and overlapping in a fan-like manner, finishing in the center.

8. Bake for 35 minutes.

9. Shortly before end of baking process, heat apricot glaze and water in small saucepan over medium heat until mixture is smooth.

10. Transfer baked pie to wire rack and immediately pour on glaze evenly. Let cool for 30 minutes and serve, or store in sealed container at room temperature for up to two days.

Tarte Tatin

This upside-down pie, which originates in France, emerges from the oven with its beautifully caramelized apples exposed.

INGREDIENTS

1 stick (4 ounces) unsalted butter

¾ cup sugar

8 Granny Smith apples, peeled, cored, and quartered

Perfect Pie Dough (page 8)

Equipment

One 8-inch heatproof pan (or skillet), plus one serving plate slightly larger than the pan

PREPARATION

1. Preheat oven to 375°F.

2. Heat butter and sugar in pan over medium heat, stirring occasionally until mixture turns golden brown color and has caramel texture.

3. Remove pan from heat and let rest 15 minutes, until mixture has cooled.

4. Arrange quartered apples in pan, starting at the edges and overlapping in a fan-like manner, finishing in the center.

5. Return pan to stove and cook on low heat for 40-50 minutes. Check occasionally to make sure liquid is barely simmering, not boiling.

6. Remove from heat and let chill for 15 minutes.

7. Working on a well-floured surface, roll out dough to a thickness of about ⅛ inch. Carefully place dough on top of cooked apples. Using sharp knife, trim excess edges of dough, roll into ball, cover with plastic wrap, and freeze for future use.

8. Bake for 25 minutes until crust turns golden brown. Carefully remove tart from oven and place serving plate (upside down) on top of crust. Quickly turn pan over (using oven mitts) onto plate. Serve immediately or store in sealed container at room temperature for up to two days. May be served with ice cream, whipped cream, or crème fraiche.

Caramel Apple Pie

The larger the apples, the easier they are to peel. So if you find big apples, cut down the number down to five. You can sprinkle a little sugar on top just before baking for a crisper, more golden pie.

INGREDIENTS

½ stick (2 ounces) unsalted butter

½ cup sugar

6 Golden Delicious apples, peeled, cored, and cut into ¼-inch cubes

1 teaspoon cinnamon

Perfect Pie Dough (page 8)

¼ cup Apricot Glaze (page 16)

2 tablespoons water

Equipment

One standard 9-inch pie plate

PREPARATION

1. Preheat oven to 375°F. Heat a large skillet over medium heat and add butter and sugar. Cook until butter melts and sugar turns a light caramel color.

2. Add cubed apples and cinnamon and cook over low heat until apples have soaked up the caramel liquid and are nearly dry (30-40 minutes).

3. Set cooked apples aside to chill. They can be prepared a day in advance and refrigerated.

4. Working on a well-floured surface, roll out dough to a thickness of about ⅛ inch.

5. Carefully place sheet of dough into pie plate, using your fingers to gently press dough into bottom and up sides. Trim excess edges of the dough, roll into ball, and put aside for making top crust.

6. Place cooked apple mixture on top of dough.

7. Working on a well-floured surface, roll out leftover dough to a thickness of about ⅛ inch. Place dough on top of cooked apple mixture. Using sharp knife, trim excess edges of dough, and gently crimp together the top and bottom layers of dough so that pie is completely sealed. With knife, make five small slits in top layer of dough.

8. Bake for 35 minutes. Shortly before end of the baking process, heat apricot glaze and water in small saucepan over medium heat until mixture is smooth.

9. Transfer baked pie to wire rack and immediately pour on glaze evenly. Let cool for 30 minutes and serve, or store in sealed container at room temperature for up to two days.

Pears in Red Wine Pie

You can use any type of pear for this recipe. The advantage of the cinnamon-brown Bosc pears is that they're available nearly year-round, and their long neck and rough skin make them easy to peel.

INGREDIENTS

10 ripe but firm pears, peeled, cored, and halved lengthwise

2 cups dry red wine

½ cup sugar

1 teaspoon cinnamon

Almond Tart Dough (page 9)

2 cups Almond Cream (page 14)

Equipment

One standard 9-inch pie plate

PREPARATION

1. Preheat oven to 375°F.

2. In a medium skillet, cook the pears, red wine, sugar, and cinnamon over medium heat until mixture comes to a boil. Lower heat and cook for 30 minutes.

3. Remove skillet from heat. Remove only the pears, place in a bowl, and chill until they reach room temperature.

4. Place skillet back on stove and cook over low heat until liquid reduces to syrup.

5. Working on a well-floured surface, roll out dough to a thickness of about ⅛-inch.

6. Carefully place sheet of dough into pie plate and gently press dough into bottom and up sides. Trim excess edges of dough, roll into ball, cover with plastic wrap, and freeze for future use.

7. Pour almond cream evenly over the dough and arrange cooked pears on top.

8. Bake for 35 minutes.

9. When thoroughly baked, remove pie from oven, place on wire rack, and immediately brush on wine syrup.

10. Let rest for 30 minutes and serve, or store in sealed container at room temperature for up to two days.

Caramelized Banana Tarts

Serves

6

This is the perfect recipe for making use of those super-ripe bananas that are nearly too soft to eat. The riper the banana, the sweeter these tarts will be. The tantalizing aroma of caramelized bananas will fill your house.

INGREDIENTS

Almond Tart Dough (page 9)

1 egg, beaten

2 cups Pastry Cream (page 11)

6 ripe bananas, cut into ¼ inch slices

¼ cup sugar

Equipment

Six 3-inch tartlet pans

Parchment paper

Pie weights or dried beans

Pastry bag with ¼-inch round tip

PREPARATION

1. Preheat oven to 375°F.

2. Working on a well-floured surface, roll out dough to a thickness of about ⅛ inch.

3. Using a 4-inch ring or large cookie cutter, cut out six circles of dough and place one in each pan, using your fingers to gently press dough into bottom and up sides. Using a fork, make several holes in dough. Trim excess edges of dough, roll into ball, cover with plastic wrap, and freeze for future use.

4. Cover pans with plastic wrap and refrigerate for 15 minutes.

5. Place a 6-inch circle of parchment paper over dough in each pan. Weight down paper with pie weights or dried beans. Bake for 20 minutes.

6. Remove pie weights or beans and parchment paper, and brush crusts with beaten egg. Bake for another 3 minutes. Remove from oven and place on wire rack until crusts reach room temperature.

7. Fill a pastry bag with pastry cream and fill crusts, starting at the edges and ending in the center. Pipe in a circular motion to achieve an even layer.

8. Arrange the banana slices evenly on top, covering all of the cream.

9. Sprinkle sugar evenly over bananas. Use kitchen torch or broiler to brown the sugar until it bubbles and darkens. Wait until bubbles subside before serving.

Apple Raisin Tart

Serve these tarts along with a warm cup of tea for a cozy autumn treat.

INGREDIENTS

½ stick (2 ounces) unsalted butter

⅓ cup sugar

6 Golden Delicious apples, peeled, cored, and sliced into eighths

½ cup raisins

1 teaspoon cinnamon

3 tablespoons berry jam (strawberry, blackberry, blueberry, or other)

Perfect Pie Dough (page 8)

¼ cup Apricot Glaze (page 16)

2 cups water

Equipment

One standard 9-inch fluted tart pan

PREPARATION

1. Preheat oven to 375°F.

2. Heat a large skillet over medium heat and add butter and sugar. Cook until butter melts and sugar turns a light caramel color.

3. Add the apples, raisins, and cinnamon to skillet and cook over low heat until apples turn a light golden brown.

4. Remove from heat, add jam, and stir until mixture is smooth. Set aside to cool. (You can prepare and refrigerate fruit and jam mixture a day in advance.)

5. Working on a well-floured surface, roll out dough to a thickness of about ⅛ inch.

6. Carefully place sheet of dough into tart pan, using your fingers to gently press dough into bottom and up sides. Trim excess edges of dough, roll into ball, cover with plastic wrap, and freeze for future use.

7. Place the apple and jam mixture on top of dough. (The fruit doesn't need to be neatly arranged).

8. Bake for 35 minutes.

9. Shortly before the end of baking process, heat the apricot glaze and water in small saucepan over medium heat until mixture is smooth.

10. Transfer baked tart to wire rack and immediately pour on glaze evenly. Let cool for 30 minutes and serve, or store in sealed container at room temperature for up to two days.

Apricot Crumble

This golden apricot crumble should be served warm and goes great with a cold scoop of ice cream. You can make it with fresh apricots when they're in season.

INGREDIENTS

Perfect Pie Dough (page 8)

1 cup Almond Cream (page 14)

One 16-oz. can of apricots in syrup, drained (or 2 cups fresh fruit)

¾ cup Crumble (page 13)

Equipment

One standard 9-inch pie plate

PREPARATION

1. Preheat oven to 375°F.

2. Working on a well-floured surface, roll out dough to a thickness of about ⅛ inch.

3. Carefully place sheet of dough into pie plate, using your fingers to gently press dough into bottom and up sides. Trim excess edges of dough, roll into ball, cover with plastic wrap, and freeze for future use.

4. Spread almond cream evenly on top of dough and place apricots on top of cream.

5. Sprinkle crumble on the apricots in one layer so that all are covered.

6. Bake for 35 minutes.

7. Transfer baked crumble to wire rack and let cool for 30 minutes. Serve immediately or store in sealed container at room temperature for up to two days.

Passion Fruit Cream Tarts

Watch your guests become obsessed with the sweet and sour flavor of this exotic dessert. The black seeds, which are completely edible, have a nice crunchy texture, giving this dish an extra element of surprise.

INGREDIENTS

Almond Tart Dough (page 9)

4 egg yolks

½ cup sugar

1 cup passion fruit purée

Equipment

Six 3-inch tartlet pans

Parchment paper

Pie weights or dried beans

Passion fruit may be found in specialty supermarkets. When ripe, it has a wrinkled, dimpled purple skin. For use in this recipe, simply cut the fruit in half and spoon out the pulp. You can leave the seeds in or remove them by straining the pulp in a non-aluminum sieve.

PREPARATION

1. Preheat oven to 375°F.

2. Working on a well-floured surface, roll out dough to a thickness of about ⅛ inch.

3. Using a 4-inch ring or large cookie cutter, cut out six circles of dough and place them in the pans, using your fingers to gently press dough into bottom and up sides. Using a fork, make several holes in dough. Trim excess edges, roll into ball, cover with plastic wrap, and freeze for future use.

4. Cover pans with plastic wrap and refrigerate for 15 minutes.

5. Place a 6-inch circle of parchment paper over dough in each pan. Weight down paper with pie weights or dried beans. Bake for 20 minutes. Remove pie weights or beans and parchment paper.

6. In a bowl, mix together eggs and sugar using a whisk. Add passion fruit pulp and stir until mixture is smooth.

7. Pour mixture over baked crusts and bake for another 20 minutes.

8. Transfer baked tarts to wire rack and let cool for 30 minutes. Serve immediately or store in sealed container at room temperature for up to two days.

Grilled Peach Tart

A great dessert for the summer months: the peaches are in season and the grilling can be done on an outdoor barbeque.

INGREDIENTS

6 fresh, still-firm peaches, pitted and sliced into eighths

Perfect Pie Dough (page 8)

1 egg, beaten

2 cups Cream Cheese Filling (page 15)

¼ cup Apricot Glaze

2 tablespoons of water

Equipment

One standard 9-inch fluted tart pan

Parchment paper

Pie weights or dried beans

Pastry bag with ⅓-inch round tip

PREPARATION

1. Preheat oven to 375°F. Heat a grill pan over high heat. When pan is very hot, place peach slices inside and cook for 4 minutes on each side, until fruit is seared with line markings from pan.

2. Set peaches aside to cool until they reach room temperature. Working on a well-floured surface, roll out dough to a thickness of about ⅛ inch.

3. Carefully place sheet of dough into tart pan, using your fingers to gently press dough into bottom and up sides. Using a fork, make several holes in dough. Trim excess edges of dough, roll into ball, cover with plastic wrap, and freeze for future use.

4. Cover pan with plastic wrap and refrigerate for 15 minutes. Place a 12-inch circle of parchment paper over dough. Weight down paper with pie weights or dried beans. Bake for 20 minutes. Remove pie weights or beans and parchment paper, brush crust with egg, and bake for another 3 minutes. Remove from oven and place on wire rack until it reaches room temperature.

5. Using pastry bag, pipe cream cheese filling into crust, starting at the edges and ending in the center. Pipe in a circular motion to achieve an even layer. Arrange grilled peaches on top of filling, starting at the edges and overlapping in a fan-like manner, finishing in the center.

6. Heat apricot glaze and water in small saucepan over medium heat until mixture is smooth and syrupy. Generously brush apricots with syrup. Chill tart in refrigerator for 30 minutes before serving. It should be served no more than 12 hours after preparation.

Mango and Coconut Cream Tarts

The best mangoes to use in this recipe are ones that are just barely ripe. They're easy to peel and their tartness is a perfect match for the sweet coconut cream.

INGREDIENTS

Almond Tart Dough (page 9)

1 egg, beaten

2 cups Coconut Cream (page 12)

2 mangos, peeled and thinly sliced

¼ cup Apricot Glaze (page 16)

2 tablespoons water

Equipment

Six 3-inch tartlet pans

Parchment paper

Pie weights or dried beans

PREPARATION

1. Preheat oven to 375°F degrees. Working on a well-floured surface, roll out dough to a thickness of about ⅛ inch.

2. Using a 4-inch ring or large cookie cutter, cut out six circles of dough and place them in the pans, using your fingers to gently press dough into bottom and up sides. Using a fork, make several holes in dough. Trim excess edges, roll into ball, cover with plastic wrap, and freeze for future use.

3. Cover pans with plastic wrap and refrigerate for 15 minutes.

4. Place a 6-inch circle of parchment paper over dough in each pan. Weight down paper with pie weights or dried beans. Bake for 20 minutes.

5. Remove pie weights or beans and parchment paper, brush dough with egg, and bake for another 3 minutes. Remove pans from oven and place on wire rack until they reach room temperature.

6. Spread coconut cream evenly on tart crusts and bake for 25 minutes. Remove baked tarts from oven and place on wire rack until they reach room temperature (about one hour).

7. Arrange sliced mangos on top of the filling, starting at the edges and overlapping in a fan-like manner, finishing in the center.

8. Heat apricot glaze and water in small saucepan over medium heat until mixture is smooth and syrupy. Brush mangos generously with syrup.

9. Chill tarts in refrigerator for 30 minutes before serving. They may be refrigerated for up to two days.

Plum Linzer Torte

Serves

8

The Linzer Torte, named for its city of origin, Linz, Austria, is the oldest-known torte in the world. It is a classic dessert in the Austrian, Hungarian, Swiss, German, and Tyrolean traditions and is most often eaten at Christmas.

INGREDIENTS

Filling

10 red plums, halved lengthwise, pitted, and sliced

¼ cup sugar

½ teaspoon vanilla extract

1 tablespoon fruit-based liqueur (Triple Sec, Peach Schnapps, or any other)

Perfect Pie Dough (page 8)

Linzer Torte Batter

1 stick (4 ounces) unsalted butter, softened

1 cup sugar

1 cup blanched almonds, finely ground

3 eggs

2½ cups all-purpose flour

1 teaspoon baking powder

Equipment

One standard 9-inch pie plate

PREPARATION

1. Preheat oven to 375°F.

2. Prepare filling: In a large bowl, mix together plums, sugar, vanilla extract, and liqueur and refrigerate for 30 minutes so that plums soak up the flavors.

3. Working on a well-floured surface, roll out dough to a thickness of about ⅛ inch.

4. Carefully place sheet of dough into pie plate, using your fingers to gently press dough into bottom and up sides. Trim excess edges of dough, roll into ball, cover with plastic wrap, and freeze for future use.

5. Prepare Linzer Torte mix: Using a hand or stand mixer, mix together butter and sugar on low speed until texture is creamy. Add almonds and eggs (one at a time) and continue to mix for two minutes on medium speed.

6. In a separate bowl, mix together flour and baking powder.

7. Gradually stir flour mixture into linzer torte batter until dough forms. Remove ball of dough from mixer, cover in plastic wrap, and refrigerate for 20 minutes.

8. Spoon plum mixture (including liquid) into dough and pour Linzer Torte mix on top of plums, covering them entirely.

9. Bake for 35 minutes.

10. Transfer baked torte to wire rack and let cool for 30 minutes. Serve immediately or store in sealed container at room temperature for up to two days.

Lemon Cream and Grape Tarts

Serves

You can use any type of grape for this recipe. I recommend champagne grapes for a classy tart to serve at a fancy dinner.

INGREDIENTS

Almond Tart Dough (page 9)

1 egg, beaten

2 cups Lemon Cream (page 14)

3 cups fresh seedless red grapes

Equipment

Six 3-inch tartlet pans

Parchment paper

Pie weights or dried beans

Pastry bag with ¼-inch round tip

PREPARATION

1. Preheat oven to 375°F.

2. Working on a well-floured surface, roll out dough to a thickness of about ⅛ inch.

3. Using a 4-inch ring or large cookie cutter, cut out six circles of dough and place them in the pans, using your fingers to gently press the dough into bottom and up sides. Using a fork, make several holes in dough. Trim excess edges of dough, roll into ball, cover with plastic wrap, and freeze for future use.

4. Cover pans with plastic wrap and refrigerate for 15 minutes.

5. Place a 6-inch circle of parchment paper over dough in each pan. Weight down paper with pie weights or dried beans. Bake for 20 minutes.

6. Remove pie weights or beans and parchment paper, brush dough with egg, and bake for another 3 minutes. Remove pans from oven and place on wire rack until they reach room temperature.

7. Fill pastry bag with lemon cream and fill crust, starting at the edges and ending in the center. Pipe in a circular motion to achieve an even layer.

8. Arrange grapes evenly to entirely cover the cream.

9. Serve immediately or refrigerate and serve up to 24 hours later.

Peach and Amaretto Cobbler

Serves

I favor amaretto for this recipe, but you can use any fruit-based liqueur you have in your pantry to bring out the cobbler's aromatic peach flavor.

INGREDIENTS

6 large ripe peaches, pitted and cut into ½-inch cubes

½ cup sugar

1 tablespoon cornstarch

1 tablespoon amaretto liqueur

Juicy Cobbler Dough (page 10)

1 tablespoon butter, softened

Equipment

Six 3-inch tartlet pans

PREPARATION

1. Preheat oven to 375°F.

2. In a large bowl, mix together peaches, sugar, cornstarch, and amaretto. Refrigerate for 30 minutes.

3. Prepare Juicy Cobbler Dough according to recipe on page 10.

4. Butter tart pans and distribute half the dough evenly in each.

5. Fill each pan ¾ full with peach and amaretto mix; then top with remaining cobbler dough.

6. Bake for 35 minutes. Serve immediately.

Nectarine Cobbler

There is no need to peel the nectarines for this recipe; their beautifully colored skin will peep out of the top of this cobbler.

INGREDIENTS

6 large ripe nectarines, pitted and cut into ½-inch cubes

⅔ cup sugar

1 tablespoon cornstarch

1 tablespoon brandy

Doughy Cobbler Dough (page 10)

1 tablespoon butter, softened

Equipment

One 12 x 8-inch baking dish

PREPARATION

1. Preheat oven to 375°F.

2. In a large bowl, mix together nectarines, sugar, cornstarch, and brandy. Refrigerate for 30 minutes.

3. Prepare Doughy Cobbler Dough according to recipe on page 10.

4. Butter baking dish and spread in half the cobbler dough evenly.

5. Place nectarine mixture in even layer on top of dough and fill rest of dish with remaining half of dough.

6. Bake for 35 minutes and serve immediately.

Pineapple and Caramel Cobbler

Serves

This cobbler is best served right out of the oven, accompanied by your favorite ice cream.

INGREDIENTS

½ stick (2 ounces) unsalted butter

½ cup sugar

1 large fresh pineapple, peeled, cut into half lengthwise, and then each half cut horizontally into ¼ inch slices

1 tablespoon fruit-based liqueur (such as sherry, triple sec, or schnapps)

Doughy Cobbler Dough (page 10)

1 tablespoon butter, softened

Equipment

One 12 x 8-inch baking dish

PREPARATION

1. Preheat oven to 375°F.

2. Heat a large skillet over medium heat and add butter and sugar. Cook until butter melts and sugar turns a light caramel color.

3. Add pineapple to skillet and cook on low heat until pineapple turns golden brown.

4. Remove skillet from heat and add liqueur. Set aside to cool, until pineapple reaches room temperature.

5. Prepare Doughy Cobbler Dough according to recipe on page 10.

6. Butter baking dish and spread in half the cobbler dough evenly. Place pineapples in even layer on top of dough and fill rest of dish with remaining half of dough.

7. Bake for 35 minutes and serve immediately.

Plum Clafoutis

Serves

Clafoutis is a baked French dessert traditionally made with cherries. I like to use Santa Rosa plums when they're in season, but any type of plum will work in this recipe.

INGREDIENTS

Filling

10 red plums, pitted and cut into ½-inch cubes

½ cup sugar

1 cup cornstarch

3 tablespoons sherry liqueur

½ teaspoon lemon zest

Clafoutis Dough

1¼ cup whole milk

⅓ cup sugar

1 tablespoon pure vanilla extract

3 eggs

4 tablespoons all-purpose flour

1 teaspoon baking powder

1 tablespoon brown sugar

½ teaspoon cinnamon

1 tablespoon butter, softened

Equipment

One 12 x 8-inch baking dish

PREPARATION

1. Preheat oven to 375°F.

2. In a large bowl, mix together plums, sugar, cornstarch, sherry, and lemon zest. Refrigerate for 30 minutes.

3. Meanwhile, using a stand or hand mixer, mix together milk, sugar, vanilla extract, and eggs on low speed.

4. In separate bowl, mix flour and baking powder. Gradually stir flour mixture into egg mixture until dough forms. Add brown sugar and cinnamon and turn off mixer.

5. Remove ball of dough from mixer, cover in plastic wrap, and refrigerate for 20 minutes.

6. Butter the baking dish and pour in plum mixture.

7. Spread clafoutis mix evenly on top of plums.

8. Bake for 35 minutes. Serve immediately.

Apple Cobbler

Serves

An easy, classic dessert that enhances any meal. This apple cobbler will please all ages!

INGREDIENTS

6 Granny Smith apples, peeled, cored and cut into ½ inch cubes

½ cup sugar

1 teaspoon cinnamon

1 tablespoon brandy

Doughy Cobbler Dough (page 10)

1 tablespoon butter, softened

Equipment

One 12 x 8-inch baking dish

PREPARATION

1. Preheat oven to 375°F.

2. In a large bowl, mix together apples, sugar, cinnamon, and brandy. Refrigerate for 30 minutes.

3. Prepare cobbler dough according to recipe on page 10.

4. Butter the baking dish and spread in half the cobbler dough evenly. Pour in apple mixture and fill the rest of dish with remaining cobbler dough.

5. Bake for 35 minutes and serve immediately.

Fresh Pineapple Pie

Serves

This pie makes a summer day even brighter, with pineapples at their absolute best. Serve it after an outdoor grilled dinner for the perfect dessert.

INGREDIENTS

Almond Tart Dough (page 9)

1 egg, beaten

2 cups Pastry Cream (page 11)

2 fresh pineapples, peeled, cut into half lengthwise, and then each half cut horizontally into ¼ inch slices

¼ cup Apricot Glaze (page 16)

2 tablespoons water

Equipment

One standard 9-inch pie plate

Parchment paper

Pie weights or dried beans

Pastry bag with ¼-inch round tip

PREPARATION

1. Preheat oven to 375°F. Working on a well-floured surface, roll out dough to a thickness of about ⅛ inch.

2. Carefully place sheet of dough into pie plate, using your fingers to gently press dough into bottom and up sides. Using a fork, make several holes in the dough. Trim excess edges of dough, roll into ball, cover with plastic wrap, and freeze for future use.

3. Cover pie plate with plastic wrap and refrigerate for 15 minutes.

4. Place a 12-inch circle of parchment paper over dough. Weight down paper with pie weights or dried beans. Bake for 20 minutes.

5. Remove the pie weights or beans and parchment paper, brush dough with egg, and bake for another 3 minutes. Remove plate from oven and place on wire rack until it reaches room temperature.

6. Using pastry bag, pipe pastry cream filling into crust, starting at the edges and ending in the center. Pipe in a circular motion to achieve an even layer.

7. Arrange pineapple slices on top of filling, overlapping in a fan-like manner.

8. Heat apricot glaze and water in small saucepan over medium heat until mixture is smooth and syrupy. Generously brush pineapples with syrup.

9. Refrigerate pie for 30 minutes before serving. It should be served no more than 12 hours after preparation.

Baked Lemon Tarts

With meringue added as a finishing touch, these delicate lemon tarts will liven any gathering.

INGREDIENTS

Almond Tart Dough (page 9)

1 egg, beaten

4 egg yolks

½ cup sugar

2 tablespoons cornstarch

1 cup lemon juice, freshly squeezed

½ cup Meringue (page 17) for decoration

Equipment

Six 3-inch tartlet pans

Parchment paper

Pie weights or dried beans

Pastry bag with ¼-inch flower tip

PREPARATION

1. Preheat oven to 375°F. Working on a well-floured surface, roll out dough to a thickness of about ⅛ inch.

2. Using a 4-inch ring or large cookie cutter, cut out six circles of dough and place them in the pans, using your fingers to gently press dough into bottom and up sides. Using a fork, make several holes in dough. Trim excess edges, roll into ball, cover with plastic wrap, and freeze for future use.

3. Cover pans with plastic wrap and refrigerate for 15 minutes. Place a 6-inch circle of parchment paper over dough in each pan. Weight down paper with pie weights or dried beans. Bake for 20 minutes.

4. Remove pie weights or beans and parchment paper, brush dough with egg, and bake for another 3 minutes. Remove pans from oven and place on wire rack until they reach room temperature.

5. Reduce oven temperature to 350°F. Meanwhile, in a large bowl, mix together the egg yolks, sugar, cornstarch, and lemon juice using a whisk.

6. Fill crusts evenly with lemon mixture. Bake for 20 minutes. Transfer pans to wire rack and let cool for 30 minutes, to room temperature.

7. Fill pastry bag with meringue and pipe meringue "kisses" in circular motion around tarts, starting at the edges and ending in the center. Just before serving, use a kitchen torch (with care) to brown meringue.

8. Serve immediately or store in refrigerator for up to two days.

Key Lime Tarts

This recipe calls for the key limes to be zested. If you don't have a zester at home, you can use the smallest holes of a regular box grater or work with a kitchen peeler to slice the zest into very thin strips.

INGREDIENTS

1 pound key limes, zested and juiced (yielding about 1 cup of juice)

½ cup water

¼ cup sugar

1 Almond Tart Dough (page 9)

1 egg, beaten

4 egg yolks

½ cup sugar

1 cup condensed milk

Equipment

Six 4x2-inch rectangular tart pans

Parchment paper

Pie weights or dried beans

PREPARATION

1. Using a zester, grate lime peels (green part only, stopping before you get to bitter, white cottony pith).

2. Cut zested limes in half and juice them, setting them aside juice for later use.

3. Fill small saucepan with water and add lime zest. Bring to a bowl, and then drain using a fine sieve. Repeat this step two more times to get rid of any remaining bitterness of the lime zest.

4. Place ½ cup of water, sugar, and lime zest in saucepan and cook over medium heat for 15-20 minutes, until liquid turns into thick syrup.

5. Remove saucepan from heat and set aside until it cools to room temperature.

6. Working on a well-floured surface, roll out dough to a thickness of about ⅛ inch.

7. Cut six 6-inch x 4-inch rectangles out of dough and place them in the pans, using your fingers to gently press dough into bottom and up sides. Using a fork, make several holes in dough. Trim excess edges of dough, roll into ball, cover with plastic wrap, and freeze for future use.

(continued on next page)

(continued from previous page)

8. Cover pans with plastic wrap and refrigerate for 15 minutes. Preheat oven to 375°F.

9. Place six 8-inch x 6-inch rectangles of parchment paper over dough. Weight down paper with pie weights or dried beans. Bake for 15 minutes. Remove pie weights or beans and parchment paper, brush dough with egg, and bake for another 3 minutes. Remove plate from oven and place on wire rack until it reaches room temperature.

10. Reduce oven temperature to 350°F.

11. Meanwhile, in a large bowl, mix together the egg yolks, sugar, condensed milk, and reserved lime juice using a whisk.

12. Pour lime juice mixture into crusts and bake for another 20 minutes.

13. Transfer pans to wire rack and let cool for 30 minutes.

14. Decorate top of each tart with 1 tablespoon of the lime zest and 1 tablespoon of the syrup. Refrigerate for an hour before serving. The tarts can be refrigerated for up to two days after preparation.

Apple and Berry Pie

The combination of sweet apples and tart berries makes for a perfect-tasting pie. Choose your favorite berries and substitute the Golden Delicious apples with Granny Smiths if you prefer a tarter flavor.

INGREDIENTS

½ stick (2 ounces) unsalted butter

⅓ cup sugar

4 Golden Delicious apples, peeled, cored, and sliced into eighths

1 teaspoon cinnamon

Perfect Pie Dough (page 8)

1 cup fresh berries (raspberry, blackberry, blueberry). If frozen, thaw and drained of excess water

¼ cup Apricot Glaze (page 16)

2 tablespoons of water

Equipment

One standard 9-inch pie plate

PREPARATION

1. Preheat oven to 375°F.

2. Heat a large skillet over medium heat and add butter and sugar. Cook until the butter melts and sugar turns a light caramel color.

3. Add apple slices and cinnamon and cook on low heat until apples turn light golden brown.

4. Set apples aside to chill. They can be prepared a day in advance and refrigerated.

5. Working on a well-floured surface, roll out dough to a thickness of about ⅛ inch.

6. Carefully place sheet of dough into pie plate, using your fingers to gently press dough into bottom and up sides. Trim excess edges dough, roll into ball, cover with plastic wrap, and freeze for future use.

7. Place cooked apple mixture into dough and add berries.

8. Bake for 35 minutes.

9. Shortly before end of baking process, heat apricot glaze and water in small saucepan over medium heat until mixture is smooth.

10. Transfer baked pie to wire rack and immediately pour on glaze evenly. Let cool for 30 minutes and serve, or store in sealed container at room temperature for up to two days.

Berries

Berry and Vanilla Cream Pie

•

Berry Crème Brûlée Tart

•

Blueberry and Lemon Cream Pie

•

Baked Strawberry Tarts

•

Strawberry and Vanilla Cream Pie

•

Spiced Berry Pie

•

Traditional Cranberry Tart

•

Cherry and White Chocolate Pie

•

Baked Strawberry Cobbler

•

Blueberry Cobbler

•

Cherry Cobbler

•

Red Currant Cobbler

•

Mixed Berry Cobbler

•

Raspberry Cobbler

•

Rhubarb and Strawberry Cobbler

•

Cranberry Cobbler

•

Mixed Berry Crumble

Berry and Vanilla Cream Pie

Choose your favorite berry for this recipe or use a combination for a particularly colorful, elegant pie.

INGREDIENTS

Perfect Pie Dough (page 8)

1 egg, beaten

2 cups Pastry Cream (page 11)

1 pound fresh berries (blackberries, blueberries, raspberries, etc.)

¼ cup Apricot Glaze (page 16)

2 tablespoons water

Equipment

One standard 9-inch pie plate

Parchment paper

Pie weights or dried beans

Pastry bag with ⅓-inch round tip

PREPARATION

1. Preheat oven to 375°F.

2. Working on a well-floured surface, roll out dough to a thickness of about ⅛ inch.

3. Carefully place sheet of dough into pie plate, using your fingers to gently press dough into bottom and up sides. Trim excess edges of dough, roll into ball, cover with plastic wrap, and freeze for future use.

4. Cover pie plate with plastic wrap and refrigerate for 15 minutes.

5. Place a 12-inch circle of parchment paper over dough. Weight down paper with pie weights or dried beans. Bake for 20 minutes.

6. Remove pie weights or beans and parchment paper, brush dough with egg, and bake for another 3 minutes. Remove plate from oven and place on wire rack until it reaches room temperature.

7. Using pastry bag, pipe pastry cream into crust, starting from the edges and ending in the center. Pipe in a circular motion to achieve an even layer.

8. Arrange fresh berries in a fan-like manner on top of filling, starting at the edges and finishing in the center.

9. Heat apricot glaze and water in small saucepan over medium heat until mixture is smooth and syrupy. Generously brush berries with syrup.

10. Refrigerate pie for 30 minutes before serving. It should be served no more than 12 hours after preparation.

Berry Crème Brûlée Tart

The beautiful berries peeping out of the rich cream makes this tart a true crowd pleaser. You can sprinkle a bit of brown sugar on top once the tart has cooled and then use a kitchen burner to brown and bubble the sugar.

INGREDIENTS

Perfect Pie Dough (page 8)

1 egg, beaten

1 cup heavy cream

4 egg yolks

½ cup powdered sugar

½ cup frozen mixed berries, thawed and drained of excess water

Equipment

One standard 9- inch fluted tart pan

Parchment paper

Pie weights or dried beans

PREPARATION

1. Preheat oven to 375°F.

2. Working on a well-floured surface, roll out dough to a thickness of about ⅛ inch.

3. Carefully place the sheet of dough into the pan, using your fingers to gently press dough into bottom and up sides. Trim excess edges of dough, roll into ball, cover with plastic wrap, and freeze for future use.

4. Cover pan with plastic wrap and refrigerate for 15 minutes.

5. Place a 12-inch circle of parchment paper over dough. Weight down paper with pie weights or dried beans. Bake for 20 minutes.

6. Remove pie weights or beans and parchment paper, brush dough with egg, and bake for another 3 minutes. Remove pan from oven and place on wire rack until it reaches room temperature.

7. Reduce oven temperature to 325° F.

8. In a large bowl, mix together the heavy cream, egg yolks, and powdered sugar using a whisk.

9. Pour liquid mixture into crust and place berries on top. Carefully place the pie in oven to bake for another 25 minutes, until liquid mixture has thickened to jelly-like consistency.

10. Transfer tart to wire rack and let cool for 30 minutes.

11. Serve immediately or store in refrigerator for up to two days.

Blueberry and Lemon Cream Pie

In our family, the kids are in charge of adding the blueberries to this pie. When it's ready, they pick them off one by one before reaching the lemon cream filling!

INGREDIENTS

Perfect Pie Dough (page 8)

1 egg, beaten

2 cups Lemon Cream (page 14)

1 pound fresh blueberries

¼ cup Apricot Glaze (page 16)

2 tablespoons water

Equipment

Six 3-inch tartlet pans

Parchment paper

Pie weights or dried beans

Pastry bag with ⅓-inch round tip

PREPARATION

1. Preheat oven to 375°F.

2. Working on a well-floured surface, roll out dough to a thickness of about ⅛ inch.

3. Using a 4-inch ring or large cookie cutter, cut out six circles of dough and place them in the pans, using your fingers to gently press dough into bottom and up sides. Trim excess edges of dough, roll into ball, cover with plastic wrap, and freeze for future use.

4. Cover pans with plastic wrap and refrigerate for 15 minutes.

5. Place a 6-inch circle of parchment paper over dough in each pan. Weight down paper with pie weights or dried beans. Bake for 20 minutes.

6. Remove pie weights or beans and parchment paper, brush dough with egg, and bake for another 3 minutes. Remove pans from oven and place on wire rack until they reach room temperature.

7. Fill pastry bag with lemon cream and fill each crust, starting from the edges and ending in the center. Pipe in a circular motion to achieve an even layer.

8. Arrange blueberries in a fan-like manner on top of lemon cream, starting at the edges and finishing in the center.

9. Heat apricot glaze and water in small saucepan over medium heat until mixture is smooth and syrupy. Generously brush blueberries with syrup.

10. Refrigerate pie for 30 minutes before serving. It should be served no more than 12 hours after preparation.

Baked Strawberry Tarts

When using a top layer of dough in a pie or tart, holes or slits need to be made so the heat doesn't get trapped inside. Be creative and look around your kitchen for a cutting device. I sometimes use a small shot glass or top of a bottle.

INGREDIENTS

1½ pounds fresh strawberries, stems removed

1 cup powdered sugar

1 tablespoon cornstarch

Perfect Pie Dough (page 8)

1 egg, beaten

¼ cup sugar, (to sprinkle on top)

Equipment

Six 3-inch tartlet pans

Parchment paper

Pie weights or dried beans

Pastry bag with ⅓-inch round tip

PREPARATION

1. Preheat oven to 375°F.

2. In large bowl, mix together the strawberries, powdered sugar, and cornstarch. Set aside for later use.

3. Working on a well-floured surface, roll out dough to a thickness of about ⅛ inch.

4. Using a 4-inch ring or large cookie cutter, cut out six circles of dough. Then cut out another six 3-inch diameter circles. You should have twelve dough circles, six one inch larger than the others.

5. Place the six larger dough circles into pans, using your fingers to gently press dough into bottom and up sides.

6. Pour strawberry mixture evenly into each pan.

7. Cut 1-inch hole in center of six smaller dough circles.

8. Place the six smaller circles on top of strawberry mixture and gently crimp together top and bottom layers of dough so that pie is sealed all the way around.

9. Mix the beaten egg and milk together in a small bowl. Brush each top layer of dough with egg mixture and sprinkle on sugar evenly. Refrigerate for 15 minutes. Bake for 30 minutes or until top of pie turns golden brown.

10. Transfer pans to wire rack and let cool for 30 minutes. Serve tarts or store in sealed container at room temperature for up to two days.

Strawberry and Vanilla Cream Pie

Serves

6

Small strawberries are best with this recipe because you can keep them whole. If you use larger ones, just cut them in half.

INGREDIENTS

Almond Tart Dough (page 9)

1 egg, beaten

2 cups pastry cream

1½ pounds fresh strawberries, stems removed

¼ cup Apricot Glaze (page 16)

2 tablespoons water

Equipment

Six 3-inch tartlet pans

Parchment paper

Pie weights or dried beans

Pastry bag with ⅓-inch round tip

PREPARATION

1. Preheat oven to 375°F.

2. Working on a well-floured surface, roll out dough to a thickness of about ⅛ inch.

3. Using a 4-inch ring or large cookie cutter, cut out six circles of dough and place them in the pans, using your fingers to gently press dough into bottom and up sides. Trim excess edges of dough, roll into ball, cover with plastic wrap, and freeze for future use.

4. Cover pans with plastic wrap and refrigerate for 15 minutes.

5. Place a 6-inch circle of parchment paper over dough in each pan. Weight down paper with pie weights or dried beans. Bake for 20 minutes.

6. Remove pie weights or beans and parchment paper, brush dough with egg, and bake for another 3 minutes. Remove pans from oven and place on wire rack until they reach room temperature.

7. Fill pastry bag with pastry cream and fill crusts with cream, starting from the edges and ending in the center. Pipe in a circular motion to achieve an even layer.

8. Arrange strawberries in a circular manner on top of cream, starting at the edges and finishing in the center.

9. Heat apricot glaze and water in small saucepan over medium heat until mixture is smooth and syrupy. Generously brush strawberries with syrup.

10. Refrigerate pie for 30 minutes before serving. It should be served no more than 12 hours after preparation.

Spiced Berry Pie

The cinnamon and nutmeg in this pie, mixed with the berries, will fill your house with a wonderful aroma that lasts for hours.

INGREDIENTS

Perfect Pie Dough (page 8)

1 egg, beaten

2 cups frozen mixed berries, thawed and drained of excess water

½ cup powdered sugar

1 teaspoon cinnamon

½ teaspoon nutmeg

Equipment

One standard 9-inch pie plate

Parchment paper

Pie weights or dried beans

PREPARATION

1. Preheat oven to 375°F.

2. Working on a well-floured surface, roll out dough to a thickness of about ⅛ inch.

3. Carefully place sheet of dough into pie plate, using your fingers to gently press dough into bottom and up sides. Trim excess edges of dough, roll into ball, cover with plastic wrap, and freeze for future use.

4. Cover pie plate with plastic wrap and refrigerate for 15 minutes.

5. Place a 12-inch circle of parchment paper over dough. Weight down paper with pie weights or dried beans. Bake for 20 minutes.

6. Remove pie weights or beans and parchment paper, brush dough with egg, and bake for another 3 minutes. Remove plate from oven and place on wire rack until it reaches room temperature.

7. In a large bowl, mix together the berries, powdered sugar, cinnamon, and nutmeg.

8. Pour berry mixture into the crust and bake for another 25 minutes.

9. Transfer pie to wire rack and let cool for 30 minutes. Serve or store in sealed container at room temperature for up to two days.

Traditional Cranberry Tart

The perfect tart for celebrating any holiday, especially Christmas. You can choose the width of the strips you use to cover the pie—thin ones to expose the cranberries or thick ones for a doughier tart.

INGREDIENTS

2 cups frozen cranberries, thawed and drained of excess water

¾ cup powdered sugar

Perfect Pie Dough (page 8)

1 egg, beaten

Equipment

One standard 9- inch fluted tart pan

Parchment paper

Pie weights or dried beans

PREPARATION

1. Preheat oven to 375°F.

2. In a large bowl, mix together the cranberries and powdered sugar. Set aside for later use.

3. Working on a well-floured surface, roll out dough to a thickness of about ⅛ inch.

4. Carefully place sheet of dough into tart pan, using your fingers to gently press dough into bottom and up sides. Trim excess edges of dough and roll out excess dough to a thickness of about ⅛ inch. Cut out four ¼-inch x 10-inch strips of dough and set them aside.

5. Pour cranberry mixture evenly into dough in pan. Place one dough strips on top of cranberry mixture, crimping edge firmly to bottom layer of dough. Give pan a quarter turn and place another dough strip on top.

6. Repeat this step with remaining strips. Make sure all strips are firmly secured to bottom layer of dough. The pie will now be divided into eight "slices."

7. Mix the beaten egg and milk together in a small bowl. Brush dough strips thoroughly with beaten egg mixture.

8. Bake for 35 minutes.

9. Transfer tart to wire rack and let cool for 30 minutes. Serve or store in sealed container at room temperature for up to two days.

Cherry and White Chocolate Pie

Serves

6

Try this recipe in early summer when cherries are ripe and you'll have a sweet and tangy pie to serve on a cool evening.

INGREDIENTS

Almond Tart Dough (page 9)

1 egg, beaten

½ cup heavy cream

1 cup white chocolate

1½ pounds fresh cherries, stems removed and pitted

¼ cup Berry Glaze (page 16)

2 tablespoons water

Equipment

Six 3-inch tartlet pans

Parchment paper

Pie weights or dried beans

Pastry bag with ⅓-inch round tip

PREPARATION

1. Preheat oven to 375°F.

2. Working on a well-floured surface, roll out dough to a thickness of about ⅛ inch.

3. Using a 4-inch ring or large cookie cutter, cut out six circles of dough and place them in the pans, using your fingers to gently press dough into bottom and up sides. Trim excess edges of dough, roll into ball, cover with plastic wrap, and freeze for future use.

4. Cover pans with plastic wrap and refrigerate for 15 minutes.

5. Place a 6-inch circle of parchment paper over dough in each pan. Weight down paper with pie weights or dried beans. Bake for 20 minutes.

6. Remove pie weights or beans and parchment paper, brush dough with egg, and bake for another 3 minutes. Remove pans from oven and place on wire rack until they reach room temperature.

7. In a small saucepan, heat heavy cream over medium heat until small bubbles appear (just before the boiling point). Remove pan from heat and add white chocolate. Using a whisk or rubber spatula, stir cream and chocolate to smooth consistency.

8. Pour chocolate and cream mixture evenly into crust, place pie on tray, and freeze for one hour.

9. Remove from freezer and arrange cherries in a circular manner on top, starting at the edges and finishing in the center.

10. Heat berry glaze and water together in a small saucepan over medium heat until mixture is smooth. Generously brush cherries with berry glaze.

11. Refrigerate pie for 30 minutes before serving. It should be served no more than 12 hours after preparation.

Baked Strawberry Cobbler

Serves

8

A cobbler topped with golden crumble makes for a beautiful and easily prepared dessert. Serve it with a scoop of your favorite ice cream.

INGREDIENTS

1 pound frozen strawberries, thawed and drained of excess water

1 cup sugar

1 tablespoon cornstarch

1 tablespoon fruit-based liqueur (such as sherry, triple sec, or schnapps)

Juicy Cobbler Dough (page 10)

1 tablespoon butter, softened

½ cup Crumble (page 13)

Equipment

One 12 x 8-inch baking dish

PREPARATION

1. Preheat oven to 375°F.

2. In a large bowl, mix together the strawberries, sugar, cornstarch, and liqueur. Set aside for 30 minutes.

3. Prepare cobbler dough according to instructions on page 10.

4. Butter the baking dish. Fill dish evenly with half the cobbler dough.

5. Fill dish ¾ full with strawberry and liqueur mixture; then fill rest of dish with remaining cobbler dough.

6. Sprinkle crumble on top. Bake for 35 minutes.

7. Serve immediately.

Blueberry Cobbler

Serves

Blueberries have proven to be a great source of antioxidants. So pick up a package of fresh (or fresh-frozen) berries and start reaping the benefits.

INGREDIENTS

1 pound blueberries (if frozen, thawed and drained of excess water)

½ cup packed brown sugar

1 tablespoon cornstarch

1 tablespoon sherry liqueur

1 teaspoon pure vanilla extract

Juicy Cobbler Dough (page 10)

1 tablespoon butter, softened

Equipment

One 12 x 8-inch baking dish

PREPARATION

1. Preheat oven to 375°F.

2. In a large bowl, mix together the blueberries, brown sugar, cornstarch, sherry liqueur and vanilla extract. Set aside for 30 minutes.

3. Prepare cobbler dough according to instructions on page 10.

4. Butter the baking dish and fill evenly with half the cobbler dough.

5. Fill baking dish ¾ full with blueberry and liqueur mixture; then fill rest of dish with remaining cobbler dough.

6. Bake for 35 minutes. Serve immediately.

Cherry Cobbler

Serves

8

Enjoy this cobbler year-round as a grand finale to any meal.

INGREDIENTS

1 pound frozen sweet cherries, thawed and drained of excess water

½ cup sugar

1 tablespoon cornstarch

3 tablespoons sherry liqueur

½ teaspoon lemon zest

Doughy Cobbler Dough (page 10)

1 tablespoon butter, softened

Equipment

One 8 x 12-inch baking dish

PREPARATION

1. Preheat oven to 375°F.

2. In a large bowl, mix together the cherries, sugar, cornstarch, sherry liqueur, and lemon zest. Set aside for 30 minutes.

3. Prepare cobbler dough according to instructions on page 10.

4. Butter the baking dish and fill evenly with half the cobbler dough.

5. Fill baking dish ¾ full with cherry mixture; then fill rest of dish with remaining cobbler dough.

6. Bake for 35 minutes. Serve immediately.

Red Currant Cobbler

Serves

8

Make this cobbler for Thanksgiving and surprise your guests by replacing the usual cranberries with exotic red currants.

INGREDIENTS

1 pound frozen red currants, thawed and drained of excess water

¾ cup packed brown sugar

1 tablespoon cornstarch

1 tablespoon vodka

½ teaspoon lemon zest

Doughy Cobbler Dough (page 10)

1 tablespoon butter, softened

Equipment

One 12 x 8-inch baking dish

PREPARATION

1. Preheat oven to 375°F.

2. In a large bowl, mix together the red currants, brown sugar, cornstarch, vodka, and lemon zest. Set aside for 30 minutes.

3. Prepare cobbler dough according to instructions on page 10.

4. Butter the baking dish and fill evenly with half the cobbler dough.

5. Fill baking dish ¾ full with red currant mixture; then fill rest of dish with remaining cobbler dough.

6. Bake for 35 minutes. Serve immediately.

Mixed Berry Cobbler

During "berry season" in the summer months, replace the frozen berries with your favorite fresh ones.

INGREDIENTS

½ pound frozen mixed berries, thawed and drained of excess water

2 Granny Smith apples, peeled, cored, and cut into ½-inch cubes

¾ cup sugar

1 tablespoon cornstarch

½ teaspoon cinnamon

1 tablespoon brandy

Doughy Cobbler Dough (page 10)

1 tablespoon butter, softened

Equipment

One 12 x 8-inch baking dish

PREPARATION

1. Preheat oven to 375°F.

2. In a large bowl, mix together the berries, apples, sugar, cornstarch, cinnamon, and brandy. Set aside for 30 minutes.

3. Prepare cobbler dough according to instructions on page 10.

4. Butter the baking dish and fill evenly with half the cobbler dough.

5. Fill baking dish ¾ full with berry and apple mixture; then fill rest of dish with remaining cobbler dough.

6. Bake for 35 minutes. Serve immediately.

Raspberry Cobbler

Serves

The velvety raspberries mixed with the aromatic sherry liqueur and tangy lemon zest make this cobbler hard to resist.

INGREDIENTS

1 pound frozen raspberries, thawed and drained of excess water

¾ cup sugar

1 tablespoon cornstarch

1 tablespoon sherry liqueur

½ teaspoon lemon zest

Juicy Cobbler Dough (page 10)

1 tablespoon butter, softened

Equipment

One 12 x 8-inch baking dish

PREPARATION

1. Preheat oven to 375°F.

2. In a large bowl, mix together the raspberries, sugar, cornstarch, sherry liqueur, and lemon zest. Set aside for 30 minutes.

3. Prepare cobbler dough according to instructions on page 10.

4. Butter the baking dish and fill evenly with half the cobbler dough.

5. Fill baking dish ¾ full with raspberry and liqueur mixture; then fill rest of dish with remaining cobbler dough.

6. Bake for 35 minutes. Serve immediately.

Rhubarb and Strawberry Cobbler

Serves

When buying rhubarb, be sure to choose fresh crisp stalks that are pinkish-red rather than green. The redder the rhubarb the sweeter the taste.

INGREDIENTS

½ stick (2 ounces) unsalted butter

1 pound rhubarb, cut into ½-inch cubes

PREPARATION

1. Preheat oven to 375°F.

2. In a small saucepan, melt the butter over medium heat. Add rhubarb.

½ cup packed brown sugar

½ pound frozen strawberries, thawed and drained of excess water

½ cup sugar

1 tablespoon cornstarch

1 tablespoon sherry liqueur

½ teaspoon lemon zest

Doughy Cobbler Dough (page 10)

1 tablespoon butter, softened

Equipment

One 12 x 8-inch baking dish

and brown sugar and cook over low heat until the rhubarb becomes soft (and can be pierced easily with a fork), 25-30 minutes.

3. Remove from heat and place rhubarb mixture into large bowl. Add the strawberries, sugar, cornstarch, sherry liqueur, and lemon zest and mix well. Set aside for 30 minutes.

4. Preheat oven to 375°F. Prepare cobbler dough according to instructions on page 10.

5. Butter the baking dish. Evenly fill the dish with half of the cobbler dough.

6. Fill baking dish ¾ full with rhubarb and strawberry mixture; then fill rest of dish with remaining cobbler dough.

7. Bake for 35 minutes. Serve immediately.

Cranberry Cobbler

Serves

8

For a more aromatic fall dessert, cut the allspice by half and add a quarter teaspoon each of ground cloves and nutmeg.

INGREDIENTS

1 pound fresh cranberries

1 cup sugar

1 tablespoon cornstarch

1 tablespoon apple liqueur

1 teaspoon allspice

Doughy Cobbler Dough (page 10)

1 tablespoon butter, softened

Equipment

One 12 x 8-inch baking dish

PREPARATION

1. Preheat oven to 375°F.

2. In a large bowl, mix together the cranberries, sugar, cornstarch, apple liqueur, and allspice. Set aside for 30 minutes.

3. Prepare cobbler dough according to instructions on page 10.

4. Butter the baking dish and fill evenly with half the cobbler dough.

5. Fill baking dish ¾ full with cranberry mixture; then fill rest of dish with remaining cobbler dough.

6. Bake for 35 minutes. Serve immediately.

Mixed Berry Crumble

A hassle-free dessert that emerges from the oven golden on the outside and juicy on the inside. What more could you ask for?

INGREDIENTS

2 pounds frozen mixed berries, thawed and drained of excess water

1 cup packed brown sugar

1 tablespoon cornstarch

1 tablespoon sherry liqueur

1 teaspoon cinnamon

3 cups Crumble (page 13)

1 tablespoon butter, softened

Equipment

One 12 x 8-inch baking dish

PREPARATION

1. Preheat oven to 375°F.

2. In a large bowl, mix together the mixed berries, sugar, cornstarch, sherry liqueur, and cinnamon. Set aside for 30 minutes.

3. Prepare crumble according to instructions on page 13.

4. Butter the baking dish and place berry mixture into dish evenly.

5. Sprinkle crumble on top of berries in one layer, covering them completely.

6. Bake for 35 minutes and serve immediately.

Nuts

Pecan Pie

•

Hazelnut and Apricot Jam Tarts

•

Roasted Peanut and Coconut Cobbler

•

Rhubarb and Almond Cobbler

•

Coconut Cream and Baked Nut Pie

•

Caramel Peanut Tarts

•

Coconut and Dulce de Leche

•

Mixed Nut Pie

•

Peanut Butter Pie

•

Almond and Chocolate Chip Cobbler

•

Walnut and Orange Marmalade Tart

•

Maple and Walnut Pie

•

Dark Chocolate Chip Cobbler

•

Baked Coconut Tarts

Pecan Pie

One of the best things about this traditional pie is that it tastes great at any temperature. It's soft and pudding-like when served warm, especially flavorful at room temperature, and candy-like when cold. Take your pick!

INGREDIENTS

Perfect Pie Dough (page 8)

2 cups pecans, chopped

½ cup packed brown sugar

1 stick (4 ounces) unsalted butter, softened

2 cups whole pecans

¼ cup Apricot Glaze (page 16)

2 tablespoons water

Equipment

One standard 9-inch pie plate

PREPARATION

1. Preheat oven to 375°F.

2. Working on a well-floured surface, roll out dough to a thickness of about ⅛ inch.

3. Carefully place sheet of dough into pie plate, using your fingers to gently press dough into bottom and up sides. Trim excess edges of dough, roll into ball, cover with plastic wrap, and freeze for future use.

4. Cover the pie plate with plastic wrap and refrigerate for 15 minutes.

5. In a large bowl, mix together the chopped pecans, brown sugar, and butter using a wooden spoon.

6. Spread pecan mixture evenly over dough. Arrange whole pecans on top in a circle, starting at the edges and ending in the center.

7. Bake for 35 minutes.

8. Shortly before end of baking process, heat apricot glaze and water in small saucepan over medium heat until mixture is smooth.

9. Transfer pie to wire rack and immediately pour on glaze evenly. Let cool for 30 minutes and serve, or store in sealed container at room temperature for up to two days.

Hazelnut and Apricot Jam Tarts

Toasting hazelnuts brings out their rich, sweet nutty flavor. For instructions see note below.

INGREDIENTS

Perfect Pie Dough (page 8)

1 egg, beaten

½ apricot jam

2 cups hazelnuts, toasted, skinned, and chopped

Equipment

Six 3-inch tartlet pans

Parchment paper

Pie weights or dried beans

Spread hazelnuts on a baking sheet and toast in a warm oven for 10-15 minutes. While they're still warm, wrap the nuts in a kitchen towel and rub the towel on your kitchen countertop vigorously until the skins are removed.

PREPARATION

1. Preheat oven to 375°F.

2. Working on a well-floured surface, roll out dough to a thickness of about ⅛ inch.

3. Using a 4-inch ring or large cookie cutter, cut out six circles of dough and place them in the pans, using your fingers to gently press dough into bottom and up sides. Trim excess edges of dough, roll into ball, cover with plastic wrap, and freeze for future use.

4. Cover pans with plastic wrap and refrigerate for 15 minutes.

5. Place a 6-inch circle of parchment paper over dough in each pan. Weight down paper with pie weights or dried beans. Bake for 20 minutes.

6. Remove pie weights or beans and parchment paper, brush dough with egg, and bake for another 3 minutes. Remove pans from oven and place on wire rack until they reach room temperature.

7. Spread on apricot jam evenly and fill rest of pans with hazelnuts. Bake for an additional 15 minutes.

8. Serve immediately or store in refrigerator in sealed container for up to two days.

Roasted Peanut and Coconut Cobbler

Serves

Peanuts, which contain more protein than any other nut, are also a treat for the palate. Serve this cobbler to your family and watch their faces light up.

INGREDIENTS

Juicy Cobbler Dough (page 10)

½ cup grated unsweetened coconut

½ cup roasted peanuts

2 tablespoons butter, softened

¼ cup sugar

1 tablespoon butter, softened

Equipment

One 12 x 8-inch baking dish

PREPARATION

1. Preheat oven to 375°F.

2. Prepare cobbler dough according to instructions on page 10.

3. In a large bowl, mix together the coconut, peanuts, butter, and sugar.

4. Butter the baking dish and spread in half the cobbler dough evenly.

5. Place half the coconut and peanut mixture in an even layer on top, and fill rest of dish with remaining cobbler dough. Sprinkle on remaining coconut and peanuts.

6. Bake for 35 minutes and serve immediately.

Rhubarb and Almond Cobbler

Serves

8

Bring out the beautiful pinkish-red color of the rhubarb by soaking the stalks in ice water for fifteen minutes before starting this recipe.

INGREDIENTS

Doughy Cobbler Dough (page 10)

2 tablespoons butter, softened

¼ cup sugar

½ pound rhubarb, cut into ½-inch cubes

½ cup almonds, peeled and coarsely chopped

1 tablespoon butter, softened

Equipment

One 12 x 8-inch baking dish

PREPARATION

1. Preheat oven to 375°F.

2. Prepare cobbler dough according to instructions on page 10.

3. In a small saucepan, heat the butter and sugar on low heat until thick syrup forms. Add rhubarb and cook for 15 minutes, stirring frequently.

4. Add almonds to saucepan and continue to cook another 10 minutes, stirring frequently. Remove pan from heat and allow cooling to room temperature.

5. Butter the baking dish and spread in half of the cobbler dough evenly. Place half the rhubarb and almond mixture in an even layer on top of cobbler dough, and fill rest of dish with remaining half of cobbler dough. Sprinkle remaining rhubarb and almonds on top.

6. Bake for 35 minutes and serve immediately.

Coconut Cream and Baked Nut Pie

Serves

8

Coconut lovers beware—this exotic nutty dessert may make you feel like you've been transported to a tropical island.

INGREDIENTS

Perfect Pie Dough (page 8)

¼ cup sugar

¼ cup boiling water

2 cups blanched sliced almonds

1 tablespoon brandy

1 cup Coconut Cream (page 12)

Equipment

One standard 9-inch pie plate

PREPARATION

1. Preheat oven to 375°F.

2. Working on a well-floured surface, roll out dough to a thickness of about ⅛ inch.

3. Carefully place sheet of dough into pie plate, using your fingers to gently press dough into bottom and up sides. Trim excess edges of dough, roll into ball, cover with plastic wrap, and freeze for future use.

4. Cover pie plate with plastic wrap and refrigerate for 30 minutes.

5. In a large bowl, mix together the sugar and water until sugar appears to have dissolved.

6. Add almonds and brandy to bowl and set mixture aside.

7. Spread coconut cream evenly over dough and top with walnut mixture. Bake for 35 minutes.

8. Transfer pie to wire rack and let cool for 30 minutes. Serve or store in sealed container at room temperature for up to two days.

Caramel Peanut Tarts

These tarts are so sticky and sweet that they resemble the inside of a Snickers bar. Don't omit the meringue. It gives the tarts the finish they deserve.

INGREDIENTS

Perfect Pie Dough (page 8)

¼ stick (2 ounces) unsalted butter

½ cup sugar

2 cups shelled and skinned peanuts

1 egg, beaten

½ cup Meringue (page 17)

Equipment

Six 3-inch tartlet pans

Parchment paper

Pie weights or dried beans

Pastry bag with ¼-inch round tip

PREPARATION

1. Preheat oven to 375°F.

2. Working on a well-floured surface, roll out dough to a thickness of about ⅛ inch.

3. Using a 4-inch ring or large cookie cutter, cut out six circles of dough and place them in the pans, using your fingers to gently press dough into bottom and up sides. Trim excess edges of dough, roll into ball, cover with plastic wrap, and freeze for future use.

4. Cover pans with plastic wrap and refrigerate for 15 minutes.

5. Meanwhile, heat a large skillet over medium heat and add butter and sugar. Cook until butter melts and sugar turns a light caramel color.

6. Add peanuts to skillet and cook over low heat for 10 minutes, stirring frequently.

7. Put skillet aside to cool. The peanuts can be prepared a day in advance and refrigerated.

8. Place a 6-inch circle of parchment paper over dough. Weight down paper with pie weights or dried beans. Bake for 20 minutes.

9. Remove pie weights or beans and parchment paper, brush dough with egg, and bake for another 3 minutes. Remove pans from oven and place on wire rack until they reach room temperature.

(continued on next page)

(continued from previous page)

10. Evenly divide peanut mixture among pans and bake for 10 minutes.

11. Transfer pans to wire rack let cool for 30 minutes, to room temperature.

12. Fill pastry bag with meringue and pipe thin lines horizontally across tarts; then pipe thin lines vertically, making a crisscross design.

13. Serve immediately or store in refrigerator in sealed container for up to two days.

Coconut and Dulce de Leche

Serves

8

A traditional Spanish, milk-based sauce, dulce de leche can be found in specialty supermarkets. Given its similarity to caramel, it can be substituted with butterscotch or caramel syrup.

INGREDIENTS

Juicy Cobbler Dough (page 10)

½ cup grated coconut

½ cup dulce de leche

1 tablespoon butter, softened

Equipment

One 12 x 8-inch baking dish

PREPARATION

1. Preheat oven to 375°F.

2. Prepare cobbler dough according to instructions on page 10.

3. Butter the baking dish and spread in half of cobbler dough evenly. Place half of coconut and half of dulce de leche in an even layer on top of cobbler dough, and fill rest of dish with remaining half of cobbler dough. Sprinkle remaining coconut and dulce de leche on top.

4. Bake for 35 minutes and serve immediately.

Mixed Nut Pie

This recipe calls for five different kinds of nuts. Use them all or substitute with others. Just make sure you have 2½ cups of nuts in all.

INGREDIENTS

Perfect Pie Dough (page 8)

½ cup walnuts, chopped

½ cup hazelnuts, chopped

½ cup pine nuts, chopped

½ cup macadamia nuts, chopped

½ cup blanched almonds, chopped

¼ cup powdered sugar

2 tablespoons boiling water

1 tablespoon brandy

½ cup raspberry jam

Equipment

One standard 9-inch pie plate

PREPARATION

1. Preheat oven to 375°F.

2. Working on a well-floured surface, roll out dough to a thickness of about ⅛ inch.

3. Carefully place sheet of dough into pie plate, using your fingers to gently press dough into bottom and up sides. Trim excess edges of dough, roll into ball, cover with plastic wrap, and freeze for future use.

4. Cover pie plate with plastic wrap and refrigerate for 15 minutes.

5. In a large bowl mix together the walnuts, hazelnuts, pine nuts, macadamia nuts, blanched almonds, powdered sugar, boiling water, and brandy using a wooden spoon.

6. Spread raspberry jam evenly over dough and top with nut mixture. Bake for 35 minutes.

7. Transfer pie to wire rack and let cool for 30 minutes. Serve or store in sealed container at room temperature for up to two days.

Peanut Butter Pie

Serves

A favorite with the younger crowd. Don't worry about the rum—it will enhance the flavor and aroma but leave no alcoholic taste or effect.

INGREDIENTS

Perfect Pie Dough (page 8)

½ cup powdered sugar

⅓ cup smooth peanut butter

2 tablespoons boiling water

1 tablespoon rum

2 cups shelled and skinned peanuts

Equipment

One standard 9-inch pie plate

PREPARATION

1. Preheat oven to 375°F.

2. Working on a well-floured surface, roll out dough to a thickness of about ⅛ inch.

3. Carefully place sheet of dough into pie plate, using your fingers to gently press dough into bottom and up sides. Trim excess edges of dough, roll into ball, cover with plastic wrap, and freeze for future use.

4. Cover pie plate with plastic wrap and refrigerate for 15 minutes.

5. In a large bowl, mix together the powdered sugar, peanut butter, boiling water, rum, and peanuts using a wooden spoon.

6. Pour peanut mixture evenly over dough. Bake for 35 minutes.

7. Transfer pie to wire rack and let cool for 30 minutes. Serve or store in sealed container at room temperature for up to two days.

Almond and Chocolate Chip Cobbler

Serves

A cobbler that's perfect for children's birthday parties but will delight the grownups as well.

INGREDIENTS

Juicy Cobbler Dough (page 10)

1 tablespoon butter, softened

½ cup blanched almonds, finely chopped

½ cup semi-sweet chocolate chips

Equipment

One 12 x 8-inch baking dish

PREPARATION

1. Preheat oven to 375°F.

2. Prepare cobbler dough according to instructions on page 10.

3. Butter the baking dish and spread in half the cobbler dough evenly. Place half the almonds and half the chocolate chips in an even layer on top, and fill rest of dish with remaining cobbler dough. Sprinkle remaining almonds and chocolate chips on top.

4. Bake for 35 minutes and serve immediately.

Walnut and Orange Marmalade Tart

Serves

8

Don't be fooled by the short ingredient list here. This tart will come out looking beautifully classy and equally as tasty. Try it for your next brunch and you'll find you have a new favorite.

INGREDIENTS

Perfect Pie Dough (page 8)

1 cup orange marmalade

2 cups walnuts, chopped

1 tablespoon brandy

Equipment

One standard 9-inch fluted tart pan

PREPARATION

1. Preheat oven to 375°F.

2. Working on a well-floured surface, roll out dough to a thickness of about ⅛ inch.

3. Carefully place sheet of dough into tart pan, using your fingers to gently press dough into bottom and up sides. Trim excess edges of dough, roll into ball, cover with plastic wrap, and freeze for future use.

4. Cover pan with plastic wrap and refrigerate for 15 minutes.

5. In a large bowl, mix together the orange marmalade, walnuts, and brandy.

6. Spread orange marmalade mixture on top of dough evenly.

7. Bake for 35 minutes.

8. Transfer tart to wire rack and let cool for 30 minutes. Serve immediately or store in sealed container at room temperature for up to two days.

Maple and Walnut Pie

This easy, minimal-ingredient recipe produces a pie that will warm up any stomach on a cold winter's day.

INGREDIENTS

Perfect Pie Dough (page 8)

3 cups walnuts, chopped

½ cup maple syrup

1 tablespoon rum

Equipment

One standard 9-inch pie plate

PREPARATION

1. Preheat oven to 375°F.

2. Working on a well-floured surface, roll out dough to a thickness of about ⅛ inch.

3. Carefully place sheet of dough into pie plate, using your fingers to gently press dough into bottom and up sides. Trim excess edges of dough, roll into ball, cover with plastic wrap, and freeze for future use.

4. Cover pie plate with plastic wrap and refrigerate for 15 minutes.

5. In a large bowl, mix together the walnuts, maple syrup, and rum using a wooden spoon.

6. Pour walnut mixture evenly over dough. Bake for 35 minutes.

7. Transfer pie to wire rack and let cool for 30 minutes. Serve or store in sealed container at room temperature for up to two days.

Dark Chocolate Chip Cobbler

Makes

This cobbler is an easy dessert to whip up when you don't have time for anything fancy or complicated.

INGREDIENTS

Doughy Cobbler Dough (page 10)

1 tablespoon butter, softened

1 cup dark chocolate chips

Equipment

One 12 x 8-inch baking dish

PREPARATION

1. Preheat oven to 375°F.

2. Prepare cobbler dough according to instructions on page 10.

3. Butter the baking dish and spread in half the cobbler dough evenly.

4. Place ½ cup of dark chocolate in an even layer on top of the dough, and fill rest of dish with remaining cobbler dough. Sprinkle on remaining dark chocolate chips.

5. Bake for 35 minutes and serve immediately.

Baked Coconut Tarts

Makes

I like to serve these tarts in small rectangular tart pans and serve them when they are still warm from the oven.

INGREDIENTS

Perfect Pie Dough (page 8)

1 cup coconut cream

½ cup dried coconut flakes

Equipment

Six 4 x 2-inch rectangular tart pans (or six 3-inch tartlet pans)

PREPARATION

1. Preheat oven to 375°F.

2. Working on a well-floured surface, roll out dough to a thickness of about ⅛ inch.

3. Cut out six 6-inch x 4-inch rectangles of dough and place them in the pans, using your fingers to gently press dough into bottom and up sides. Trim excess edges of dough, roll into ball, cover with plastic wrap, and freeze for future use.

4. Place two tablespoons of coconut cream in each pan. Bake for 30 minutes.

5. Transfer pans to wire rack and let cool for 30 minutes.

6. Decorate top of each tart with 1 tablespoon coconut flakes and serve. The tarts can be stored in sealed container at room temperature for up to two days.

Chocolate

Mint Chocolate Pie

•

Milk Chocolate and Berry Jam Pie

•

Chocolate Cream Tarts

•

White Chocolate and Blueberry Pie

•

Chocolate Mousse Pie

•

Dark Chocolate Pie

•

Milk Chocolate, Almonds and Caramel Pie

•

Chocolate Macadamia Pie

•

Dark Chocolate and Coconut Pie

•

Mississippi Mud Pie

Mint Chocolate Pie

Serves

8

Turn the kids' favorite ice cream, Mint Chocolate Chip, into one of their favorite pies.

INGREDIENTS

Perfect Pie Dough (page 8)

1 egg, beaten

2 cups dark chocolate

1 cup heavy cream

2 tablespoons fresh mint leaves, finely chopped

Equipment

One standard 9-inch pie plate

Parchment paper

Pie weights or dried beans

PREPARATION

1. Preheat oven to 375°F.

2. Working on a well-floured surface, roll out dough to a thickness of about ⅛ inch.

3. Carefully place sheet of dough into pie plate, using your fingers to gently press dough into bottom and up sides. Trim excess edges of dough, roll into ball, cover with plastic wrap, and freeze for future use.

4. Cover pie plate with plastic wrap and refrigerate for 15 minutes.

5. Place a circle 12-inch circle of parchment paper over dough. Weight down paper with pie weights or dried beans. Bake for 20 minutes.

6. Remove pie weights or beans and parchment paper, brush dough with egg, and bake for another 3 minutes. Remove plate from oven and place on wire rack until it reaches room temperature.

7. Place the chocolate, heavy cream, and mint in a heatproof bowl. Set bowl over saucepan of gently simmering water, stirring occasionally, until chocolate is melted and mixture is smooth. Remove bowl from pan of water.

8. Pour chocolate mixture into crust and freeze for one hour.

9. The pie may be served after an hour in freezer or stored in refrigerator for up to two days.

Milk Chocolate and Berry Jam Pie

Serves

Use any type of berry jam you have in your pantry (strawberry, raspberry, blackberry, etc.) for this easy-to-make pie.

INGREDIENTS

Perfect Pie Dough (page 8)

1 egg, beaten

2 cups milk chocolate

1 cup heavy cream

½ cup berry jam

Equipment

One standard 9-inch pie plate

Parchment paper

Pie weights or dried beans

PREPARATION

1. Preheat oven to 375°F.

2. Working on a well-floured surface, roll out dough to a thickness of about ⅛ inch.

3. Carefully place sheet of dough into pie plate, using your fingers to gently press dough into bottom and up sides. Trim excess edges of dough, roll into ball, cover with plastic wrap, and freeze for future use.

4. Cover pie plate with plastic wrap and refrigerate for 15 minutes.

5. Place a 12-inch circle of parchment paper over dough. Weight down paper with pie weights or dried beans. Bake for 20 minutes.

6. Remove pie weights or beans and parchment paper, brush dough with egg, and bake for another 3 minutes. Remove plate from oven and place on wire rack until it reaches room temperature.

7. Place chocolate and heavy cream in a heatproof bowl. Set bowl over saucepan of gently simmering water, stirring occasionally, until chocolate is melted and mixture is smooth. Remove bowl from pan of water.

8. Spread berry jam on crust in an even layer. Pour chocolate mixture over jam and freeze for one hour.

9. The pie may be served after an hour in freezer or stored in refrigerator for up to two days.

Chocolate Cream Tarts

For Valentine's Day, I like to make these chocolate cream tarts in heart-shaped tartlet pans, but you can make them all year round using six regular tartlet pans.

INGREDIENTS

Perfect Pie Dough (page 8)

1 egg, beaten

2 cups dark chocolate, plus ¼ cup grated (for decoration)

1 cup heavy cream

1 tablespoon brandy

Equipment

Six 3-inch tartlet pans

Parchment paper

Pie weights or dried beans

PREPARATION

1. Preheat oven to 375°F.

2. Working on a well-floured surface, roll out dough to a thickness of about ⅛ inch.

3. Using a 4-inch ring or large cookie cutter, cut out six circles of dough and place them in the pans, using your fingers to gently press the dough into bottom and up sides. Trim excess edges of dough, roll into ball, cover with plastic wrap, and freeze for future use.

4. Cover pans with plastic wrap and refrigerate for 15 minutes.

5. Place a 6-inch circle of parchment paper over dough in each pan. Weight down paper with pie weights or dried beans. Bake for 20 minutes.

6. Remove pie weights or beans and parchment paper, brush dough with egg, and bake for another 3 minutes. Remove pans from oven and place on a wire rack until they reach room temperature.

7. Place chocolate and heavy cream in a heatproof bowl. Set bowl over saucepan of gently simmering water, stirring occasionally, until chocolate is melted and mixture is smooth. Add brandy and mix well. Remove bowl from pan of water.

8. Pour chocolate mixture into crust. Freeze for one hour.

9. Remove pie from freezer and decorate with grated chocolate. Serve immediately or store in refrigerator for up to two days.

White Chocolate and Blueberry Pie

Serves

10

This creamy pie is great for special occasions. It's easy to make and always comes out rich and tart, delighting all taste buds.

INGREDIENTS

Perfect Pie Dough (page 8)

1 egg, beaten

2 cups white chocolate

½ cup heavy cream

½ pound fresh blueberries

Equipment

One standard 9-inch pie plate

Parchment paper

Pie weights or dried beans

PREPARATION

1. Preheat oven to 375°F.

2. Working on a well-floured surface, roll out dough to a thickness of about ⅛ inch.

3. Carefully place sheet of dough into pie plate, using your fingers to gently press dough into bottom and up sides. Trim excess edges of dough, roll into ball, cover with plastic wrap, and freeze for future use.

4. Cover pie plate with plastic wrap and refrigerate for 15 minutes.

5. Place a 12-inch circle of parchment paper over dough. Weight down paper with pie weights or dried beans. Bake for 20 minutes.

6. Remove pie weights or beans and parchment paper, and brush dough with egg, and bake for another 3 minutes. Remove plate from oven and place on wire rack until it reaches room temperature.

7. Place white chocolate and heavy cream in a heatproof bowl. Set bowl over saucepan of gently simmering water, stirring occasionally until chocolate is melted and mixture is smooth. Remove bowl from pan of water.

8. Pour white chocolate mixture into crust. Freeze for one hour. Remove pie from freezer and decorate pie with blueberries, starting from the rim and ending up in the center.

9. Serve immediately or store in refrigerator for up to two days.

Chocolate Mousse Pie

This rich chocolate mousse pie is for true chocolate lovers. Earn yourself a place in their hearts by making it for them.

INGREDIENTS

Perfect Pie Dough (page 8)

1 egg, beaten

1 cup dark chocolate, plus ¼ cup grated (for decoration)

½ cup heavy cream

1 tablespoon dark rum

3 egg whites

½ cup sugar

Equipment

One standard 9-inch pie plate

Parchment paper

Pie weights or dried beans

PREPARATION

1. Preheat oven to 375°F. Working on a well-floured surface, roll out dough to a thickness of about ⅛ inch.

2. Carefully place sheet of dough into pie plate, using your fingers to gently press dough into bottom and up sides. Trim excess edges of dough, roll into ball, cover with plastic wrap, and freeze for future use.

3. Cover pie plate with plastic wrap and refrigerate for 15 minutes. Place a 12-inch circle of parchment paper over dough. Weight down paper with pie weights or dried beans. Bake for 20 minutes.

4. Remove pie weights or beans and parchment paper, brush dough with egg, and bake for another 3 minutes. Remove plate from oven and place on a wire rack until it reaches room temperature.

5. Place chocolate and heavy cream in a heatproof bowl. Set bowl over saucepan of gently simmering water, stirring occasionally, until chocolate is melted and the mixture is smooth. Add rum and mix well. Remove bowl from pan of water.

6. Using a stand or hand mixer, whisk egg whites on high speed and gradually add sugar until egg whites are stiff but not dry. Fold egg whites into chocolate mixture until combined.

7. Carefully pour chocolate and egg white mixture into crust. Freeze for one hour. Remove pie from freezer and sprinkle grated chocolate on top. Serve immediately or store in refrigerator for up to two days.

Dark Chocolate Pie

Serves

8

A rich, dark chocolate pie that spoils your guests with something really special. Be sure to let the refrigerated pie come to room temperature before you serve it.

INGREDIENTS

Perfect Pie Dough (page 8)

2 cups dark chocolate

½ stick (2 ounces) unsalted butter

1 tablespoon brandy

½ cup sugar

3 eggs

1 tablespoon powdered sugar (for decoration)

Equipment

One standard 9-inch pie plate

PREPARATION

1. Preheat oven to 375°F.

2. Working on a well-floured surface, roll out dough to a thickness of about ⅛ inch.

3. Carefully place sheet of dough into pie plate, using your fingers to gently press dough into bottom and up sides. Trim excess edges of dough, roll into ball, cover with plastic wrap, and freeze for future use.

4. Cover pie plate with plastic wrap and refrigerate for 15 minutes.

5. Place chocolate and butter in a heatproof bowl. Set bowl over saucepan of gently simmering water, stirring occasionally, until chocolate is melted and mixture is smooth.

6. Remove bowl from pan of water. Add brandy and sugar. Add the eggs, one at a time, stirring constantly so they don't become cooked.

7. Pour chocolate mixture into crust. Bake for 35 minutes.

8. Transfer pie to wire rack and let cool for 30 minutes.

9. Before serving, sprinkle top of pie with powdered sugar. Serve at room temperature and store in refrigerator for up to two days.

Milk Chocolate, Almonds and Caramel Pie

Serves

8

A candy bar turned pie, this sweet and crunchy treat will definitely satisfy anyone's sweet tooth.

INGREDIENTS

Perfect Pie Dough (page 8)

1 egg, beaten

1 cup milk chocolate

½ cup heavy cream

¼ cup Caramel Sauce (page 12)

1 cup whole blanched almonds

Equipment

One standard 9-inch pie plate

Parchment paper

Pie weights or dried beans

PREPARATION

1. Preheat oven to 375°F.

2. Working on a well-floured surface, roll out dough to a thickness of about ⅛ inch.

3. Carefully place sheet of dough into pie plate, using your fingers to gently press dough into bottom and up sides. Trim excess edges of dough, roll into ball, cover with plastic wrap, and freeze for future use.

4. Cover pie plate with plastic wrap and refrigerate for 15 minutes.

5. Place a circle 12-inch circle of parchment paper over dough. Weight down paper with pie weights or dried beans. Bake for 20 minutes.

6. Remove pie weights or beans and parchment paper, brush dough with egg, and bake for another 3 minutes. Remove plate from oven and place on wire rack until it reaches room temperature.

7. Place chocolate and heavy cream in a heatproof bowl. Set bowl over saucepan of gently simmering water, stirring occasionally, until chocolate is melted and mixture is smooth.

8. Pour chocolate mixture into crust and freeze for one hour.

9. Remove pie from freezer and pour on caramel sauce. Sprinkle almonds on top. Freeze for another 20 minutes.

10. Serve immediately or store in refrigerator for up to two days.

Chocolate Macadamia Pie

I find the combination of dark chocolate and macadamia nuts irresistible; but you can substitute with any type of nut you prefer.

INGREDIENTS

Perfect Pie Dough (page 8)

1 egg, beaten

2 cups dark chocolate

1 cup heavy cream

1 cup macadamia nuts, crushed

Equipment

One standard 9-inch pie plate

Parchment paper

Pie weights or dried beans

PREPARATION

1. Preheat oven to 375°F.

2. Working on a well-floured surface, roll out dough to a thickness of about ⅛ inch.

3. Carefully place sheet of dough into pie plate, using your fingers to gently press dough into bottom and up sides. Trim excess edges of dough, roll into ball, cover with plastic wrap, and freeze for future use.

4. Cover pie plate with plastic wrap and refrigerate for 15 minutes.

5. Place a 12-inch circle of parchment paper over dough. Weight down paper with pie weights or dried beans. Bake for 20 minutes.

6. Remove pie weights or beans and parchment paper, brush dough with egg, and bake for another 3 minutes. Remove plate from oven and place on wire rack until it reaches room temperature.

7. Place chocolate and heavy cream in a heatproof bowl. Set bowl over saucepan of gently simmering water, stirring occasionally, until chocolate is melted and mixture is smooth. Mix in macadamia nuts.

8. Pour chocolate mixture into crust and freeze for one hour.

9. Serve immediately or store in refrigerator for up to two days.

Dark Chocolate and Coconut Pie

To top this elegant pie, you can grate the chocolate with a regular box grater or create long, curly strips with a vegetable peeler.

INGREDIENTS

Perfect Pie Dough (page 8)

2 cups dark chocolate, plus ¼ cup grated (for decoration)

½ stick (2 ounces) unsalted butter

1 tablespoon dark rum

1 cup Coconut Cream (page 12)

Equipment

One standard 9-inch pie plate

PREPARATION

1. Preheat oven to 375°F.

2. Working on a well-floured surface, roll out dough to a thickness of about ⅛ inch.

3. Carefully place sheet of dough into pie plate, using your fingers to gently press dough into bottom and up sides. Trim excess edges of dough, roll into ball, cover with plastic wrap, and freeze for future use.

4. Cover pie plate with plastic wrap and refrigerate for 15 minutes.

5. Place chocolate and butter in a heatproof bowl. Set bowl over saucepan of gently simmering water, stirring occasionally, until chocolate is melted and mixture is smooth.

6. Remove bowl from pan of water. Add rum and coconut cream and stir until mixture is smooth.

7. Pour chocolate mixture into dough. Bake for 35 minutes.

8. Transfer pie to a wire rack and let cool for 30 minutes.

9. Before serving, sprinkle top of pie with grated chocolate. Serve at room temperature or store in refrigerator for up to two days.

Mississippi Mud Pie

Serves

8

This ultimate chocolate lovers' pie has its roots in the Deep South. Legend has it that the pie's name derives from its resemblance to the banks of the Mississippi River.

INGREDIENTS

Perfect Pie Dough (page 8)

1 cup dark chocolate

1 stick (4 ounces) unsalted butter

¼ cup maple syrup

½ cup packed brown sugar

3 eggs

¼ cup powdered sugar (for decoration)

Equipment

One standard 9-inch pie plate

PREPARATION

1. Preheat oven to 375°F.

2. Working on a well-floured surface, roll out dough to a thickness of about ⅛ inch.

3. Carefully place sheet of dough into pie plate, using your fingers to gently press dough into bottom and up sides. Trim excess edges of dough, roll into ball, cover with plastic wrap, and freeze for future use.

4. Cover pie plate with plastic wrap and refrigerate for 15 minutes.

5. Place chocolate and butter in a heatproof bowl. Set bowl over saucepan of gently simmering water, stirring occasionally, until chocolate is melted and mixture is smooth.

6. Remove bowl from pan of water. Add maple syrup and brown sugar. Add eggs, one at a time, stirring constantly so they don't become cooked.

7. Pour chocolate mixture into crust. Bake for 35 minutes.

8. Transfer pie to wire rack and let cool for 30 minutes.

9. Before serving, sprinkle top of pie with powdered sugar. Serve at room temperature or store in refrigerator for up to two days.

Cheese and More

Cheesecake and Brownie Pie

•

Pineapple Cheesecake Pie

•

Ricotta, Almond and Amaretto Pie

•

Dark Chocolate Cheesecake Pie

•

Dark Chocolate and Cream Cheese Tarts

•

Traditional Pumpkin Pie

•

Carrot Cobbler

•

Carrot and Raisin Tarts

Cheesecake and Brownie Pie

Serves

8

You can use store-bought brownies for this recipe or put in the extra effort and make your own at home. Your effort will be rewarded when you taste the difference.

INGREDIENTS

4 eggs, separated, plus 1 whole beaten egg

½ cup sugar

1 package (8 oz.) cream cheese

½ teaspoon pure vanilla extract

1 tablespoon cornstarch

Perfect Pie Dough (page 8)

1 cup store-bought brownies, cut into cubes

Equipment

One standard 9-inch pie plate

Parchment paper

Pie weights or dried beans

PREPARATION

1. Preheat oven to 375°F. Using a stand or hand mixer, whisk egg whites on high speed and gradually add sugar until whites are stiff but not dry.

2. In a separate bowl, mix together the egg yolks, cream cheese, vanilla extract, and cornstarch. Gently fold egg whites into cheese mixture using rubber spatula until mixture is smooth. Keep mixture refrigerated until ready to use.

3. Working on a well-floured surface, roll out dough to a thickness of about ⅛ inch.

4. Carefully place sheet of dough into pie plate, using your fingers to gently press dough into bottom and up sides. Trim excess edges of dough, roll into ball, cover with plastic wrap, and freeze for future use.

5. Cover pie plate with plastic wrap and refrigerate for 15 minutes. Place a 12-inch circle the parchment paper over dough. Weight down paper with pie weights or dried beans. Bake for 20 minutes.

6. Remove pie weights or beans and parchment paper, brush dough with beaten egg, and bake for another 3 minutes. Remove plate from oven and place on a wire rack for 15 minutes.

7. Reduce oven temperature to 350°F. Remove cream cheese and egg mixture from refrigerator and pour mixture into crust. Sprinkle on brownie cubes evenly.

8. Bake for 40 minutes. Transfer pie to wire rack and allow it to cool completely (about one hour).

9. Serve or refrigerate in sealed container for up to two days.

Pineapple Cheesecake Pie

Serves

8

This rich and tangy cheesecake pie is a delightful way to cap off your next backyard summer dinner.

INGREDIENTS

Perfect Pie Dough (page 8)

4 eggs, separated, plus 1 whole beaten egg

½ cup sugar

1 package (8 oz.) cream cheese

½ teaspoon pure vanilla extract

1 tablespoon cornstarch

1 cup canned pineapple cubes, drained

Equipment

One standard 9-inch pie plate

Parchment paper

Pie weights or dried beans

PREPARATION

1. Preheat oven to 375°F. Working on a well-floured surface, roll out dough to a thickness of about ⅛ inch.

2. Carefully place sheet of dough into pie plate, using your fingers to gently press dough into bottom and up sides. Trim excess edges of dough, roll into ball, cover with plastic wrap, and freeze for future use. Cover pie plate with plastic wrap and refrigerate for 15 minutes.

3. Place a circle 12-inch circle of parchment paper over dough. Weight down paper with pie weights or dried beans. Bake for 20 minutes.

4. Meanwhile, using a stand or hand mixer, whisk egg whites on high speed and gradually add sugar until whites are stiff but not dry.

5. In a separate bowl, mix together the egg yolks, cream cheese, vanilla extract, and cornstarch. Gently fold egg whites into cheese mixture using rubber spatula until mixture is smooth. Keep mixture refrigerated until ready to use.

6. Remove pie weights or beans and parchment paper. Brush dough with beaten egg, and bake for another 3 minutes. Remove plate from oven and place on wire rack for 15 minutes.

7. Reduce oven temperature to 350°F. Remove cream cheese and egg mixture from refrigerator and pour half of mixture evenly into crust. Place pineapple cubes on top of mixture and fill crust with rest of cream cheese and egg mixture.

8. Bake for 40 minutes. Transfer pie to wire rack and allow it to cool completely (about one hour). Serve or refrigerate in sealed container for up to two days.

Ricotta, Almond and Amaretto Pie

Serves

8

A delicious pie that works well as the featured item at an afternoon brunch, along with a cup of hot tea.

INGREDIENTS

Perfect Pie Dough (page 8)

4 eggs, separated, plus 1 whole beaten egg

½ cup sugar

1 cup fresh ricotta cheese

½ teaspoon pure vanilla extract

1 tablespoon cornstarch

1 cup blanched whole almonds, finely ground

½ cup sliced almonds

1 tablespoon amaretto liqueur

Equipment

One standard 9-inch pie plate

Parchment paper

Pie weights or dried beans

PREPARATION

1. Preheat oven to 375°F. Working on a well-floured surface, roll out dough to a thickness of about ⅛ inch.

2. Carefully place sheet of dough into pie plate, using your fingers to gently press dough into bottom and up sides. Trim excess edges of dough, roll into ball, cover with plastic wrap, and freeze for future use.

3. Cover pie plate with plastic wrap and refrigerate for 15 minutes. Place a 12-inch circle the parchment paper over dough. Weight down paper with pie weights or dried beans. Bake for 20 minutes.

4. Meanwhile, using a stand or hand mixer, whisk egg whites on high speed and gradually add sugar until whites are stiff but not dry.

5. In a separate bowl, mix together the egg yolks, ricotta cheese, vanilla extract, cornstarch, ground almonds, and amaretto. Gently fold egg whites into the cheese mixture using a rubber spatula until mixture is smooth. Keep mixture refrigerated until ready to use.

6. Remove pie weights or beans and parchment paper, brush dough with beaten egg, and bake for another 3 minutes. Remove pie from oven and place on a wire rack for 15 minutes. Sprinkle almond slices evenly on top.

7. Reduce oven temperature to 350°F. Remove ricotta cheese and egg mixture from refrigerator and pour mixture into crust. Sprinkle almond slices evenly on top.

8. Bake for 40 minutes. Transfer pie to wire rack allow it to cool completely (about one hour). Serve or refrigerate in sealed container for up to two days.

Dark Chocolate Cheesecake Pie

Serves

8

A pie for chocolate lovers and for cheesecakes lovers in one dessert! Serve with your favorite ice cream and no one will be able to resist this one.

INGREDIENTS

Perfect Pie Dough (page 8)

Cheese Filling

4 eggs, separated

½ cup sugar

1 package (8 oz.) cream cheese

½ teaspoon pure vanilla extract

1 tablespoon cornstarch

Dark Chocolate Filling

1 cup dark chocolate

½ stick (2 ounces) unsalted butter

1 tablespoon brandy

¼ cup sugar

3 eggs

Equipment

One standard 9-inch pie plate

PREPARATION

1. Preheat oven to 375°F. Working on a well-floured surface, roll out dough to a thickness of about ⅛ inch.

2. Carefully place the sheet of dough into the pie plate, using your fingers to gently press dough into bottom and up sides. Trim excess edges of dough, roll into ball, cover with plastic wrap, and freeze for future use.

3. Cover pie plate with plastic wrap and refrigerate for 15 minutes. Meanwhile, using a stand or hand mixer, whisk egg whites on high speed and gradually add sugar until egg whites are stiff but not dry.

4. In a separate bowl, mix together the egg yolks, cream cheese, vanilla extract, and cornstarch. Gently fold egg whites into cheese mixture using a rubber spatula until mixture is smooth. Keep mixture refrigerated until ready to use.

5. Place chocolate and butter in a heatproof bowl. Set bowl over saucepan of gently simmering water, stirring occasionally, until chocolate is melted and mixture is smooth.

6. Remove bowl from pan of water. Add brandy and sugar. Add eggs, one at a time, stirring constantly so they don't become cooked.

7. Reduce oven temperature to 350°F. Remove cream cheese and egg batter from refrigerator and pour batter into crust. Pour dark chocolate mixture on top and use table knife to swirl it through the cream cheese batter.

8. Bake for 40 minutes. Transfer pie to wire rack, allow cooling completely (about one hour). Serve or refrigerate in sealed container for up to two days.

Dark Chocolate and Cream Cheese Tarts

Serves

6

For the brave at heart only: To check whether beaten egg whites have reached the desired degree of stiffness, hold the bowl upside-down over your head. If they are stiff enough, you will stay totally clean!

INGREDIENTS

Perfect Pie Dough (page 8)

1 egg, beaten and another 2 eggs, whites only

2 cups dark chocolate

1 cup heavy cream

1 tablespoon brandy

½ cup sugar

½ package (4 oz.) cream cheese

1 teaspoon pure vanilla extract

½ teaspoon orange zest

Equipment

Six 3-inch tartlet pans

Parchment paper

Pie weights or dried beans

Pastry bag with ¼-inch round tip

PREPARATION

1. Preheat oven to 375°F.

2. Working on a well-floured surface, roll out dough to a thickness of about ⅛ inch.

3. Using a 4-inch ring or large cookie cutter, cut out six circles of the dough, and place them in the pans, using your fingers to gently press dough into bottom and up sides. Trim excess edges of dough, roll into ball, cover with plastic wrap, and freeze for future use.

4. Cover pans with plastic wrap and refrigerate for 15 minutes.

5. Place a 6-inch circle of the parchment paper over dough. Weight down paper with pie weights or dried beans. Bake for 20 minutes.

6. Remove pie weights or beans and parchment paper, brush dough with whole beaten egg, and bake for another 3 minutes. Remove pans from oven and place on wire rack until they reach room temperature.

7. Place chocolate and heavy cream in a heatproof bowl. Set bowl over saucepan of gently simmering water, stirring occasionally, until chocolate is melted and mixture is smooth. Remove bowl from pan of water and add brandy.

8. Pour chocolate mixture evenly into each pan. Freeze pans for one hour.

(continued on page 134)

(continued from page 132)

9. Meanwhile, using a stand or hand mixer, whisk egg whites on high speed and gradually add sugar until whites are stiff but not dry. Turn off mixer and fold in cream cheese, vanilla extract, and orange zest.

10. Transfer cheese and egg white mixture to pastry bag and refrigerate for 15 minutes.

11. Remove tarts from freezer after an hour. Using pastry bag filled with cream cheese and egg white mixture, pipe "kisses" in a circular motion around tarts, starting with the edges and ending in the center.

12. Serve or store in refrigerator in sealed container for up to two days.

Traditional Pumpkin Pie

8

Serve this pie with a scoop of whipped cream to each of your Thanksgiving Day guests. They will be sure to show you thanks.

INGREDIENTS

Perfect Pie Dough (page 8)

2 cups canned pumpkin

½ heavy cream

½ cup packed brown sugar

1 tablespoon cinnamon

½ teaspoon ground ginger

½ teaspoon ground cloves

3 eggs, plus one beaten egg

½ teaspoon salt

Equipment

One standard 9- inch deep-dish pie plate

Parchment paper

Pie weights or dried beans

PREPARATION

1. Preheat oven to 375°F.

2. Working on a well-floured surface, roll out dough to a thickness of about ⅛ inch.

3. Carefully place sheet of dough into pie plate, using your fingers to gently press dough into bottom and up sides. Trim excess edges of dough, roll into ball, cover with plastic wrap, and freeze for future use.

4. Cover pie plate with plastic wrap and refrigerate for 15 minutes. Place a 12-inch circle of parchment paper over dough. Weight down paper with pie weights or dried beans. Bake for 20 minutes.

5. In a large bowl, mix together the pumpkin, heavy cream, brown sugar, cinnamon, ginger, and cloves using a whisk. Add 3 eggs and salt and mix until mixture is smooth. Refrigerate batter until needed.

6. Remove pie weights or beans and parchment paper, brush dough with beaten egg, and bake for another 3 minutes. Remove from oven and place on a wire rack for 15 minutes.

7. Reduce oven temperature to 350°F.

8. Remove pumpkin batter from refrigerator and pour evenly into crust.

9. Bake for 40 minutes.

10. Transfer pie to wire rack and allow to cool completely (about one hour).

11. Serve or refrigerate in sealed container for up to two days.

Carrot Cobbler

Serves

6

Less sweet than your standard cobbler, this spiced carrot version is sure to be a hit even with a picky crowd.

INGREDIENTS

½ stick (2 ounces) unsalted butter

½ cup sugar

8 carrots, peeled and cut into ¼-inch cubes

1 teaspoon ground allspice

1 teaspoon cinnamon

Juicy Cobbler Dough (page 10)

1 tablespoon butter, softened

Equipment

Six 3-inch tartlet pans

PREPARATION

1. Preheat oven to 375°F.

2. Heat a large skillet over medium heat and add butter and sugar. Cook until butter melts and sugar turns a light caramel color.

3. Add carrots, allspice, and cinnamon and cook over low heat for about 15 minutes, stirring frequently, until carrots have softened.

4. Remove skillet from heat and allow carrots to reach room temperature (at least 30 minutes). The carrots can be prepared a day in advance and refrigerated.

5. Prepare cobbler dough according to instructions on page 10.

6. Butter tartlet pans. Fill evenly with half of cobbler dough.

7. Fill pans ¾ full with carrot mixture and top with remaining cobbler dough.

8. Bake for 35 minutes. Serve immediately.

Carrot and Raisin Tarts

Carrots are full of beta-carotene, nutrients, and anti-oxidants—good enough reason to bake these tarts and serve them to your family.

INGREDIENTS

Perfect Pie Dough (page 8)

½ stick (2 ounces) unsalted butter

⅓ cup sugar

7 carrots, peeled and cut into ½-inch cubes

1 teaspoon cinnamon

1 egg, beaten

½ cup dark raisins

Equipment

Six 3-inch tartlet pans

Parchment paper

Pie weights or dried beans

Pastry bag with ¼-inch round tip

PREPARATION

1. Preheat oven to 375°F. Working on a well-floured surface, roll out dough to a thickness of about ⅛ inch.

2. Using a 4-inch ring or large cookie cutter, cut out six circles out of dough, and place them in the pans, using your fingers to gently press dough into bottom and up sides. Trim excess edges of dough, roll into ball, cover with plastic wrap, and freeze for future use. Cover pans with plastic wrap and refrigerate for 15 minutes.

3. Heat a large skillet over medium heat and add butter and sugar. Cook until butter melts and sugar turns a light caramel color.

4. Add carrots and cinnamon and cook over low heat until carrots turn golden brown (about 15 minutes).

5. Remove skillet from heat and allow carrots to reach room temperature. The carrots can be prepared a day in advance and refrigerated,

6. Place a 6-inch circle of parchment paper over dough in each pan. Weight down paper with pie weights or dried beans. Bake for 20 minutes.

7. Remove pie weights or beans and parchment paper, brush dough with egg, and bake for another 3 minutes. Remove tartlets from oven and place on a wire rack until they reach room temperature.

8. Place carrot mixture evenly in each pan. Sprinkle raisins evenly on top of each pan. Bake for 15 minutes.

9. Transfer tartlets to wire rack and let cool for 30 minutes. Serve or store in sealed container at room temperature for up to two days.

Tips, Tools, and Ingredients

PIES

• The most important general rule in making a pie is to follow the dough preparation instructions precisely. If the dough is mediocre, the pie will be mediocre. Read all recipe instructions thoroughly before getting started.

• The basic ingredients for making dough are flour, fat, and liquids. For the fat, I prefer butter because of its rich flavor. You may also use shortening, vegetable oils, and nut oils, or a mixture of butter and oils. Liquids (water, milk, juice, heavy cream, eggs, etc.) must be cold and added gradually (eggs one at a time, for example). Always add a pinch of salt to enhance flavor.

• The ratio of basic ingredients should be as follows: one part flour, two parts fat, one part liquid, and a pinch of salt.

• All dough-making ingredients must be very cold because the dough will warm up as you work with it.

• To ensure a crisp crust, it is very important not to overwork the dough. Overworking is the main culprit of a tough crust.

• During preparation, particularly when the dough feels soft, it is wise to let it chill in the refrigerator for 30 minutes between steps. This will bring the dough "back to life" and keep it from becoming too elastic.

• When rolling out the dough, flour the top and bottom well so that it doesn't stick to the work surface or rolling pin.

• After rolling out the dough, brush off the excess flour.

• Be very gentle when transferring the dough to the pie or tart pan. Never pull or stretch the dough since that will cause it to shrink during baking.

• When pre-baking (or blind-baking) a crust, add parchment paper and pie weights or dried beans (such as kidney beans or garbanzo beans) so the dough will take the shape of the pan. Fit the parchment paper securely into the dough.

• After pre-baking a crust, remove the weights or beans three minutes before the end of the baking process, brush the crust with a beaten egg, and return it to the oven to finish baking. This step "seals" the crust from the liquid filling, keeping it flaky and crisp.

• To keep the sides of the crust from over-browning, especially after pre-baking, cover them with aluminum foil for the pre-baking stage.

• Using a baking stone will help the pie bake uniformly. The stone spreads the heat evenly through the oven, and the pie bakes inside and out in an even manner.

• If you cover your pie with a top layer of crust, cut slits or holes on top to serve as a steam vent. You can make decorative holes with a shaped cookie cutter, and you can decorate around the holes with scraps of dough shaped into leaves, hearts, flowers, etc.

• Any pie with a top layer (including strips of dough) should be brushed before baking with a beaten egg mixed with one tablespoon of milk or water. This gives the pie a nice golden color.

• To give a pie a vibrant, just-baked look, brush it after baking with a fruit-based glaze or sprinkle on powdered sugar after cooling.

• Any pie can be covered with either a top layer or strips of dough (thick or thin, according to your preference). This book contains mostly uncovered pies since I like to show off the color and texture of the pie filling.

• Shaved or melted chocolate, meringue, or candied citrus peel can be used to decorate any pie. Use your imagination to create your own decoration!

• Tasty cookies can be made from leftover scraps of dough. After rolling out the dough, cut it into any shape you want for your cookies. Brush with a beaten egg and bake at 375°F for 12-15 minutes, until just golden. You can top the egg wash with chopped nuts, grated coconut, cinnamon, or brown sugar to make a custom cookie.

COBBLERS

• The first rule of thumb when baking cobblers is to follow recipe's instructions for adding the ingredients. All of the dry ingredients should be mixed together in a bowl and set aside. All of the wet ingredients should be mixed together in a separate bowl. The dry ingredients should be gradually mixed into the wet ingredients so that no lumps form.

• Set aside the prepared cobbler batter to rest for at least 20 minutes before baking to give the ingredients (especially the baking powder) time to react.

• In fruit cobbler recipes, mix the fruit with sugar to "marinate" it for at least 30 minutes before use. The sugar will bring out the liquids in the fruit, making for an aromatic and juicy dessert. A small amount of liqueur added to a fruit cobbler will make it even more aromatic.

- In cobbler recipes calling for a juicy filling, such as berries, sprinkle brown sugar or streusel on top for a crisp, golden crust.

- Cobblers, unlike pies or cakes, should be served right out of the oven. So prepare the fillings beforehand and keep them refrigerated. Bake only when you are ready to serve.

- Choosing a baking dish is an important part of cobbler-making since they are always served right out of the dish. The nicer the dish, the nicer the cobbler.

TOOLS

- Baking stone: Baking stones are handy for any baked goods (not only sweets but pizzas and breads as well). A baking stone can be used anytime a cookie sheet is called for in a recipe. Keeping a baking stone on your oven floor at all times soaks up moisture, leaves your baked goods crispier, and prevents burning. Keep in mind that baking stones should be well heated first to work properly; preheat them for at least 30 minutes before starting to bake.

- Pie weights: Pie weights are used when pre-baking (or blind-baking) the dough before adding the filling. You can buy pie weights (usually ceramic balls or linked steel beads) in specialty cooking shops. You can substitute with a bag of dried beans or rice that are already in your pantry. Keep the bag in an air-tight container and use it the next time you pre-bake a crust.

- Pastry bags: Also known as piping bags, these can be purchased at specialty cooking shops, along with the different tips that go along with them. If your recipe calls for a pastry bag but you choose not to make a special design, you can fill an average-size zip-lock bag with your favorite topping, cut a hole in one corner, and pipe away!

- Kitchen torch: Another great tool for those who love to bake and cook. Kitchen torches, available at specialty cooking shops, can turn a tasty dessert into a beautiful, golden work of art. In most cases, you can use a preheated broiler in recipes that call for a kitchen torch.

- Heat-proof baking dishes: This book calls for several types of heat-proof baking dishes.

9-inch pie plate: Pyrex or ceramic, the ideal dish for baking pies.

9-inch deep dish pie plate: Deeper than a regular pie plate, so you will need to increase the fillings listed in this book by a quarter.

9-inch fluted tart pan: Usually ceramic or metal. Some have removable bottoms that allow you to remove the tart and serve it on any platter you wish.

Tartlet dishes: Most of the tartlet recipes in this book call for six 3-inch tartlet dishes. You can replace the tartlet dishes (without changing the recipe) with a 9-inch fluted tart pan. The advantage of tartlet dishes is that you can serve individual desserts to your guests.

- Electric hand or stand mixer: Although all recipes in the book can be made by hand (including the dough recipes), baking is usually easier and cleaner with an electric mixer. Just be sure to use the right attachment:

Wire whip: great for whipping airy mixtures such as egg whites

Dough hook: mixes and kneads yeast dough

Flat beater: mixes pastry dough while scraping the sides of the bowl, incorporating all ingredients

MAIN INGREDIENTS

- Flour: All recipes in the book call for all-purpose flour. To measure, scoop it out of a flour bag or jar using a measuring cup so that the flour mounts over the top of the cup. Sweep the back of a knife across the top of the measuring cup to level the flour. All types of flour should be stored in tightly sealed containers (I like to use wide containers for easy scooping) in a cool, dry cupboard.

- Butter: None of the recipes here that call for butter should be replaced with anything else! The best butter to use is unsalted; if you can't find it, substitute with salted. When a recipe calls for very cold butter, it should be just that. You'll taste the difference in the finished product.

- Sugar: The sugar to use for these recipes is granulated sugar, unless another (brown, powdered or confectioner's) is mentioned. All sugar should be store in tightly sealed containers in a cool, dry cupboard.

- Salt: Although it may seem an odd addition to sweet dishes, salt actually brings out all the flavors. So don't leave it out!

- Heavy cream: Also called whipping cream, heavy cream should have a milk fat content of 35-40%. Always store heavy cream in the refrigerator until use since very cold cream produces the best results.

Metric Equivalents

The recipes that appear in this cookbook use the standard United States method for measuring liquid and dry or solid ingredients (teaspoons, tablespoons, and cups). The information on this chart is provided to help cooks outside the U.S. successfully use these recipes. All equivalents are approximate.

METRIC EQUIVALENTS FOR DIFFERENT TYPES OF INGREDIENTS

A standard cup measure of a dry or solid ingredient will vary in weight depending on the type of ingredient. A standard cup of liquid is the same volume for any type of liquid. Use the following chart when converting standard cup measures to grams (weight) or milliliters (volume).

Standard Cup	Fine Powder (ex. flour)	Grain (ex. rice)	Granular (ex. sugar)	Liquid Solids (ex. butter)	liquid (ex. milk)
1	140 g	150 g	190 g	200 g	240 ml
¾	105 g	113 g	143 g	150 g	180 ml
⅔	93 g	100 g	125 g	133 g	160 ml
½	70 g	75 g	95 g	100 g	120 ml
⅓	47 g	50 g	63 g	67 g	80 ml
¼	35 g	38 g	48 g	50 g	60 ml
⅛	18 g	19 g	24 g	25 g	30 ml

USEFUL EQUIVALENTS FOR DRY INGREDIENTS BY WEIGHT

(To convert ounces to grams, multiply the number of ounces by 30.)

1 oz	=	¹⁄₁₆ lb	=	30 g
4 oz	=	¼ lb	=	120 g
8 oz	=	½ lb	=	240 g
12 oz	=	¾ lb	=	360 g
16 oz	=	1 lb	=	480 g

USEFUL EQUIVALENTS FOR LENGTH

(To convert inches to centimeters, multiply the number of inches by 2.5.)

1 in				=	2.5 cm			
6 in	=	½ ft		=	15 cm			
12 in	=	1 ft		=	30 cm			
36 in	=	3 ft	=	1 yd	=	90 cm		
40 in				=	100 cm	=	1 m	

USEFUL EQUIVALENTS FOR DRY INGREDIENTS BY WEIGHT

¼ tsp				=	1 ml	
½ tsp				=	2 ml	
1 tsp				=	5 ml	
3 tsp	=	1 tbls		½ fl oz =	15 ml	
		2 tbls	= ⅛ cup =	1 fl oz =	30 ml	
		4 tbls	= ¼ cup =	2 fl oz =	60 ml	
		5 ⅓ tbls	= ⅓ cup =	3 fl oz =	80 ml	
		8 tbls	= ½ cup =	4 fl oz =	120 ml	
		10 ⅔ tbls	= ⅔ cup =	5 fl oz =	160 ml	
		12 tbls	= ¾ cup =	6 fl oz =	180 ml	
		16 tbls	= 1 cup =	8 fl oz =	240 ml	
		1 pt	= 2 cups =	16 fl oz =	480 ml	
		1 qt	= 4 cups =	32 fl oz =	960 ml	
				= 33 fl oz =	1000 ml	= 1 liter

USEFUL EQUIVALENTS FOR COOKING/OVEN TEMPERATURES

	Fahrenheit	Celsius	Gas Mark
Freeze Water	32° F	0° C	
Room Temperature	68° F	20° C	
Boil Water	212° F	100° C	
Bake	325° F	160° C	3
	350° F	180° C	4
	375° F	190° C	5
	400° F	200° C	6
	425° F	220° C	7
	450° F	230° C	8
Broil			Grill

Index